# eat well, feel well

# eat well, feel well

more than 150 delicious

**specific carbohydrate diet**™–compliant

recipes

## kendall conrad

 THREE RIVERS PRESS
NEW YORK

# to my family

This book contains recipes for meals to help manage common digestive disorders. It is not intended as a substitute for the advice and care of your physician, and you should use proper discretion, in consultation with your physician, in utilizing the information presented. The author and the publisher expressly disclaim responsibility for any adverse effects that may result from the use or application of the information contained in this book.

Library of Congress Cataloging-in-Publication Data

Conrad, Kendall.
    Eat well, feel well : more than 150 delicious specific carbohydrate diet–compliant recipes / Kendall Conrad.
        p. cm.
    Includes index.
    1. Carbohydrates in human nutrition.   2. Monosaccharides.   3. Cookery.
I. Title.
TX553.C28 C66 2006
641.5'6383–dc22

2006015144

ISBN  978-0-307-59060-2

Printed in the United States of America

Design by Maggie Hinders
Photographs by Luca Trovato

10 9 8 7 6

First Paperback Edition

# contents

# a note from the author

**in the fall of 2004,** I began a journey that would forever change my life. The events leading up to my decision to write *Eat Well, Feel Well* are contained in the book's introduction, but I could never have imagined the profound effect that this book would have on my life after it was published.

I began to receive a handful of e-mails sent to my website EatWellFeelWelltheBook.com. Gradually, the number grew to four or five a day, and letters began coming in from people around the country who had read my book, discovered the benefits of the Specific Carbohydrate Diet, and wanted to share their stories of success. These are people who for years had suffered from IBS, Crohn's disease, autism, celiac disease, or diverticulitis, or had a son, daughter, husband, or wife who was coping with one of these afflictions.

The most unexpected and rewarding surprise for me was the heartfelt gratitude I received from these readers. Each and every one of these letters told a tale of the relief and joy that came from finally eating again without pain or sickness. What a wonderful feeling it was to know that by sharing my knowledge of cooking with the SCD, I was making a difference. What a pleasure it was to pass on the knowledge I had learned from my mentor and friend, Elaine Gottschall, author of *Breaking the Vicious Cycle*. These thank-you letters were a greater reward than any I could have imagined when I sat down to create my recipes.

In the five years since I began writing *Eat Well, Feel Well*, the world has become a very different place. Attitudes about healthy eating, alternative diets, and the benefits of gluten- and wheat-free diets have drastically changed, as millions of people seek solutions and cures beyond traditional, and sometimes ineffective, medicinal practices. Talk shows, radio broadcasts, and bookstores are now filled with authors, experts, and celebrities championing the ideas inherent in an SCD lifestyle. More and more people—and not only those with acute problems—are discovering that by eliminating certain foods from their diet they are increasing their energy and overall quality of life. There is, quite simply, a revolution taking place as people discover that they have the power to help and heal themselves.

I hope that this edition of *Eat Well, Feel Well* will reach an even greater number of people who are looking for answers and solutions to their digestion problems. This book can be the first step toward a new life—a better life—filled with the enormous benefits that come from pursuing a healthy lifestyle.

# foreword

**how wonderful the feeling!** A mother who played the important part of leading her child to a life of good health by feeding her child food fit for a king!

It's not that Kendall Conrad was a stranger to gourmet cooking—she wasn't. But when children are not well, their appetites are picky, and they seem to be addicted to the worst of foods. Parents are so concerned about getting something, *anything,* into their bodies that they often let children eat whatever they want . . . until things get really bad. Then the intelligent parent takes action.

Kendall was lucky. She found a good nutritionist who recognized the science of the Specific Carbohydrate Diet™—a balanced diet with smart carbohydrates, good proteins and fat, and lots of vitamins and minerals necessary for good health. The diet was also designed to be therapeutic for those with damaged digestive systems, so Kendall had her wish: She went back to her gourmet cooking but customized it to conform to the principles that would heal her child's body.

*Eat Well, Feel Well* is a journey into beautiful cookery that will gladden the hearts of kitchen artists everywhere, but it is also a journey back to the way we were meant to eat.

—Elaine Gottschall, M.Sc., author of *Breaking the Vicious Cycle*
Ontario, Canada
January 2005

# preface

**several years ago,** a client told me about a friend who had cured herself of Crohn's disease using a special diet created by Elaine Gottschall that eliminated all grains. As a nutritionist I was surprised, because I had always regarded whole grains, especially brown rice, as balancing, neutral, and somewhat soothing to the gastrointestinal tract. Nonetheless, I bought Gottschall's book, which featured her Specific Carbohydrate Diet. I found it fascinating. It made a strong case against grains and complex carbohydrates in certain situations—if the intestines were unable to digest them properly.

Shortly thereafter, a new client came to see me who suffered from colitis. She had been following a macrobiotic program and eventually eliminated all foods from her diet except for brown rice, in the hope that it would relieve her symptoms. But just the opposite was happening, and this woman was getting much worse.

I immediately suggested that she consider Gottschall's program. After a few weeks on the plan she was greatly improved. I was impressed. Talk is cheap when it comes to miraculous cures and special diets, but experience is worth its weight in gold. And so the SCD program became an important resource if a client needed it. I found that most of my clients who suffered from an irritated bowel were able to heal with more modified versions of the program once we discovered and removed the underlying cause, whether it was parasites or allergies to certain foods.

Then Kendall Conrad brought her daughter to see me. It appeared that large amounts of antibiotics from the child's past had created a very unbalanced stomach environment, where her absorption and gut immunity were severely compromised. We tried several approaches to restoring her digestive health but, unfortunately, created only temporary improvements. Finally, there was nothing left to do but direct Kendall to the Gottschall program, which she embraced like a tornado, and her daughter finally started showing wonderful results.

The rest is history. Her child's digestive health is completely restored, and Kendall has become a creative nutritional resource when it comes to preparing foods that kids and adults both love and are also healthy and healing for them. Her success has inspired me to do my own creative homework, to combine the guidelines of Gottschall's SCD program with the highest-nutrient foods available, empowering healing and regenerative results for many more of my clients. I am grateful to Elaine Gottschall for her vision and exploration and for making this important information available. I'm also grateful to Kendall Conrad for translating it into wonderful tasty and nutritious recipes that provide a way for others to enhance this powerful program with enjoyment and ease.

–Dale Figtree, Ph.D., Nutritionist
Santa Barbara, California
March 2006

# preface

**the intestine is a constantly evolving organ.** It is responsible for absorbing all of the nutrients that nourish the body and, at the same time, disposing all of the body's waste. It is a giant filter so sophisticated in its function that it is able to adapt to all sorts of changes in diet, environment, and stress.

Bacteria are meant to live in the intestine, but only certain types and only in limited numbers. When the balance is off, the intestine cannot do its job properly and important nutrients fail to be absorbed. In a growing child the consequence can be dramatic.

Kendall Conrad came to my pediatric practice after her daughter had developed a bacterial infection in her bowel. She had taken antibiotics to treat the infection, but the antibiotics caused even more disequilibrium, so that in the end the delicate balance of bacteria and cells lining her intestines was thoroughly disrupted. She developed difficulty absorbing most of the foods she had eaten up to this point, things that had never before caused a problem for her.

Kendall worked endlessly to find a diet that would help restore the normal balance in her daughter's intestinal tract. And then she took it a step further, writing this book to help other people who find themselves in the same position. *Eat Well, Feel Well* is written with a combination of nutritional soundness and immaculate style. Most important, it provides recipes for health that can actually heal the intestine.

> –Cara Familian Natterson, M.D.,
> author of *Your Newborn: Head to Toe*
> and *Your Toddler: Head to Toe*
> Santa Monica, California
> March 2006

# introduction

## it all started with ear infections.

From the age of six months, my youngest child suffered from one ear infection after another. I resisted giving her antibiotics and would instead try natural remedies, but to no avail. With my poor baby crying in pain, I gave in to the doctor's insistence on prescribing antibiotics because he told me that if the infection didn't clear up, my daughter could burst an eardrum or even lose her hearing. She had five of these infections by the time she was ten months old, at which point she had surgery to help drain her ears. The operation was a big success, and the good news was that she no longer had any ear infections.

Her stomach was not so fortunate, however. The antibiotics had wreaked havoc on her gut. Her immunity had been so weakened by these powerful medicines that I believe it made her more susceptible to bacteria and infections. And little did I know at the time that the food she was eating was encouraging the growth of harmful bacteria in her digestive system, making her even more susceptible to diseases and parasites.

When she was one year old, she contracted a salmonella infection and had to be hospitalized, where she was given more antibiotics. The following summer she contracted *dientamoebus fragilis,* another parasite, and was prescribed more strong medication.

At the same time she developed digestive problems. She wasn't growing properly or absorbing nutrients. She was so skinny and frail that I felt something must be seriously wrong. I kept taking her to see different doctors, hoping to find someone or something that would help her. This went on for more than a year.

Then I met a Santa Barbara, California, nutritionist named Dale Figtree. After I described my problem, she urged me to read Elaine Gottschall's *Breaking the Vicious Cycle.* I raced through the book in one night, fascinated by Gottschall's scientific research and eager to learn more about the Specific Carbohydrate Diet (SCD) she had designed to alleviate the symptoms of digestive disorders. She explained in her book that millions of people around the world suffer from gut problems and that most doctors routinely prescribe antibiotics and steroids which, for the most part, don't work.

Dale suggested I begin preparing meals for my daughter using the SCD guidelines. I had to embrace a completely different way of cooking. So many foods that I viewed as healthy ingredients—including brown rice and tofu—turned out to be dangerous for my child. Soon after I committed to this new way of cooking, which eliminated virtually all starch and complex sugars, my daughter started to feel much better, and she began to grow. Now, several years later, she's thriving.

Elaine is a miracle worker! A true pioneer and scientist, she spent her life teaching others how to heal by prescribing changes in diet and nutrition, not drugs. Her book has sold more than one million copies and has helped so many people in addition to my daughter. For more information and to read about personal success stories and testimonials, visit the official Web site at www.breakingtheviciouscycle.info.

Tested for more than fifty years by Dr. Sidney Hass and Elaine Gottschall, the Specific Carbohydrate Diet has produced very convincing results. Gottschall claims that, based on clinical study and anecdotal feedback, at least 75 percent of those who follow the diet rigidly have experienced "significant improvement."

It seems as if everyone I meet has digestive challenges or knows of someone who has digestive challenges. The SCD has been shown to help not just one segment of this population, but people with digestive illnesses that include irritable bowel syndrome, colitis, Crohn's disease, celiac disease, diabetes, *candida,* and diverticulitis, as well as many food-related allergies, acid reflux disease, indigestion, heartburn, and gas. It also appears to help children diagnosed with autism, a group of disorders that is very often accompanied by serious intestinal problems.

The best news is that this diet is a better way for *everyone* in your family to eat. The food tastes great, and it is so much easier for our bodies to digest. Foods without starch and sugar make you feel energized and healthy, and eating in this revolutionary way can help prevent digestive problems later. I believe that this approach to eating is the diet of the future.

I have always been a cook and have loved cooking. The SCD offered me challenges by limiting and editing what ingredients I could use. I accepted these challenges and began experimenting with different ways of cooking that appealed to both my family and me. *Eat Well, Feel Well* is the result of my search to create delicious, healthy recipes that my whole family would love and that range from weeknight casual to dinner party elegant. These nearly two hundred recipes will allow you to follow the dietary restrictions of

Gottschall's program *without* feeling restricted by a severely limited eating plan. I hope to show you how to incorporate SCD eating into your family's lifestyle with ease, grace, and creativity.

I encourage you to always choose the best-quality ingredients available. Invest in buying local, seasonal organic food. Try cooking with grass-fed beef and lamb that hasn't been inoculated with antibiotics and hormones. It tastes better *and* is better for you. Look for wild fish (not farm-raised) caught in clean waters and buy poultry that is free-range and organic. Visit your local farmer's market for fresh organic fruits and vegetables, and try to stay away from prepared or packaged foods as much as possible, since they usually contain large amounts of sugar, salt, starch, and preservatives.

I'm not a doctor, nutritionist, or famous chef, just a mother on a quest to heal her child and keep her family healthy. I've learned to cook as nutritiously and deliciously as possible, and I want to share what I've learned with you. In this cookbook I hope you will find more than tasty, nourishing recipes; my dream is that through it Elaine Gottschall's revolutionary approach to nutrition will reach more people in search of relief, prevention, and enduring wellness.

# about the specific carbohydrate diet

**a roll call of common digestive disorders,** including Crohn's disease, ulcerative colitis, inflammatory bowel disease, diverticulitis, celiac disease, and those associated with cystic fibrosis and some forms of autism, has caused an epidemic that affects nearly five million children and adults in the United States alone. These diseases can afflict anyone at any age. And while they are rarely fatal, they can make everyday life a misery. These illnesses have been treated with medication, surgery, and a variety of dietary campaigns, but few of these approaches have been successful over the long term . . . until recently.

Along with thousands of others, I have discovered a crucial nutrition program called the Specific Carbohydrate Diet. When strictly followed, it leaves those suffering from the above-mentioned afflictions symptom-free—in many cases for the first time in years. The difference in quality of life is extraordinary.

Biochemist Elaine Gottschall's best-selling book, *Breaking the Vicious Cycle,* initiated this global revolution; it explains how the Specific Carbohydrate Diet works and why. But not until now has there been a truly inspired cookbook designed to give readers both the kind of varied food they need to live healthy lives and the celebratory cuisine they desire that conforms strictly to the diet's specifications. In order to fully comprehend the diet and all it offers, I encourage you to read *Breaking the Vicious Cycle* as soon as possible. However, in order to understand the approach to the recipes in this book, I will outline the plan's dietary requirements as my family and I live by them.

The Specific Carbohydrate Diet includes only very specific carbohydrates—those that require minimal digestive processes, are well absorbed, and leave virtually nothing to encourage microbial overgrowth in the intestine. Foods are permitted in the program based on the way they affect body chemistry. Carbohydrates are selected or omitted because of their molecular structure.

The simpler the structure of the carbohydrate, the more easily the body digests and absorbs it. Monosaccharides (single molecules including glucose, fructose, and galactose) require no splitting by digestive enzymes in order to be absorbed by the body. They have a single-molecule structure that allows them to be easily absorbed by the intestine wall. These are the sugars we rely on in the diet. They include those found in fruits, honey, some vegetables, and a special Homemade Yogurt (page 27).

Disaccharides (double sugar molecules such as lactose, sucrose, maltose, and isomaltose) and polysaccharides (most starches) should generally be avoided. Gottschall explains that "the complex carbohydrates that are not easily digested feed harmful bacteria in our intestines, causing them to overgrow, producing by-products and inflaming the intestine wall. The diet works by starving out these bacteria and restoring the balance of bacteria in our gut." In a healthy person these bacteria exist in a state of balance in the gut, while in a person afflicted with a digestive disorder, they do not.

To elaborate on what happens: When carbohydrates are not fully digested and absorbed, they remain in the gut and become nutrition for the microbes we host. The microbes digest the unused carbohydrates through fermentation, leaving unpleasant and even dangerous waste products behind—gases such as methane, carbon dioxide, and hydrogen; lactic and acetic acids; and various toxins. Not only do these render sufferers incredibly uncomfortable but they can also irritate and damage the gut.

Bacteria in the small intestine usually trigger a worsening cycle of gas and acid production, which further inhibits absorption. The gases and acids can damage the mucosal layer of the small intestine, which then involves injury to the microvilli, the last barrier between the nutrition we take in and our bloodstream. When absorption is inhibited, folic acid and vitamin $B_{12}$ deficiency follows, and the vicious cycle spirals on, seriously damaging and possibly ulcerating the digestive organs. Other symptoms of malabsorbtion include chronic diarrhea, which depletes the body of nutrition and water necessary for good health.

So what should you eat to avoid these problems? The following list will provide you with a sense of which foods are allowed and which are discouraged on the SCD.

## MEAT AND FISH

**allowed:** All beef, lamb, pork, poultry, fresh fish, fish canned in oil or water (both are fine), and shellfish

**not allowed:** Processed meats, smoked meats (many of these products contain starch, whey, lactose, or sucrose), and breaded fish

## VEGETABLES

**allowed:** All varieties of fresh or frozen (with no added sugar or starch)
**not allowed:** Potatoes, sweet potatoes, yams, okra, jícama, seaweed, canned vegetables, and jarred vegetables with additives

## GRAINS AND LEGUMES

**allowed:** Dried beans, including navy, kidney, black beans, lentils, and split peas (allowed once you have been on the SCD for three months or are symptom-free; be sure to soak the beans for twenty-four hours before cooking to remove any excess starch)
**not allowed:** Wheat, couscous, barley, corn, rye, oats, rice, buckwheat, millet, spelt, and cereals, flours, or other products made from any of these (such as pasta and bread)

## FRUITS

**allowed:** Fresh, raw, cooked, frozen with no added sugar, dried, or canned in own juice
**not allowed:** Any fruit with sugar added or coated with a sugar-based product

## DAIRY

**allowed:** Eggs; hard, aged cheeses; farmer cheese (dry-curd cottage cheese–also known as "hoop cheese"); butter; Homemade Yogurt (page 27; a special yogurt that diminishes the growth of harmful bacteria by increasing the amount of good bacteria in the gut)
**not allowed:** Fluid milk of any kind; dried milk solids; commercial buttermilk; sour cream; commercial yogurt (because it is not properly fermented); soft fresh cheeses (such as cottage cheese and fresh mozzarella)

## NUTS

**allowed:** Unsalted nuts with or without the shell; natural nut butters (no additives or sugar); almond flour (which is simply finely ground almonds, not a grain)
**not allowed:** Shelled peanuts or mixed nuts that are roasted with a starch coating; commercial peanut butter with sweeteners and additives

## BEVERAGES AND CONDIMENTS

**allowed:** Dry wine; clear alcohol such as vodka and gin; canned tomato juice; freshly squeezed orange, grapefruit, lemon, and lime juices; apple cider without added sweetener; mint or weak black tea or coffee; corn, safflower, olive, sunflower, coconut, and soybean oils; unflavored gelatin; honey (preferably raw)

**not allowed:** Champagne; sherry; beer; rum; liqueurs; soft drinks and diet soft drinks; canned tomato sauce, paste, or puree with sugar added; any juices made from concentrate; soy milk; instant or decaffeinated tea and coffee

The research that produced the Specific Carbohydrate Diet suggests that this way of eating is right for us because it is *species appropriate.* The foods allowed on the diet are for the most part the ones that our earliest ancestors ate before agriculture began. This "original diet" that evolved over millions of years is based primarily on meat, fish, eggs, vegetables, nuts, and low-sugar fruits. This is directly opposite of our current way of eating, which is only about ten thousand years old and which prominently features starches, grains, pasta, legumes, and breads.

Gottschall points out that "in the last hundred years the increase in complex sugars and chemical additives in the diet has led to a huge increase in health problems ranging from severe bowel disorders to obesity and brain function disorders." She adds that the reason so many people experience digestive problems is that "we have not adapted to eat this modern diet, as there has not been enough time for natural selection to operate. It therefore makes sense to eat the diet we evolved with."

The nearly two hundred recipes featured in this book have been formulated and tested based on approved SCD foods. They are prepared with only "legal" sugars and starches, and feature a wide variety of proteins, vegetables, fruits, breakfast foods, desserts, beverages, and even "mock starches." Plus, there is a chapter specifically for kids that will be sure to satisfy even the pickiest eaters. This companion cookbook will allow those in search of intestinal relief to enjoy eating again and to look forward to sitting down to delicious meals with their family.

# stocking your kitchen

**as any mom or home cook knows,** it is helpful when making meals to have a well-stocked pantry, fridge, and freezer. This is even more important for those following the SCD; you can be prepared and not tempted to eat foods that should be avoided. The foods listed below are all SCD appropriate, and many are essential to both the diet and the recipes in this book.

Always try to buy organic produce, meats, fish, and other food products whenever possible. These foods, grown without pesticides, are better for you than conventional foods and taste better, too. When purchasing packaged food, be sure to read all labels very carefully. Be on the lookout for foods with hidden unwanted ingredients. Do not buy anything that contains gums, starches, or sugars (see page 29 for their names) in the ingredient list because these are not allowed on the eating plan.

Most of the foods listed below can be purchased at major supermarkets, health food stores, and gourmet markets.

## PANTRY ITEMS

**A VARIETY OF OILS** including extra-virgin olive oil, safflower oil, toasted sesame oil, and coconut oil (which is excellent for high-heat cooking and is known to be healing for the gut)

**CHICKEN STOCK** (Imagine brand is organic and has no starches or sugars added)

**VEGETABLE STOCK** (Pacific brand is organic and has no starches or sugars added)

**BALSAMIC VINEGAR** (aged eighteen years or more so that it has no excess sugars)

**RED WINE VINEGAR** (with no sugar added)

**BROWN RICE VINEGAR** (with no sugar added; Spectrum makes a good one that is also organic)

**APPLE CIDER VINEGAR**

**CAPERS IN OLIVE OIL**

**ITALIAN-BRAND CANNED WHOLE TOMATOES AND SUN-DRIED TOMATO PASTE** (with no sugars or starches added; unlike American law, Italian law mandates that all ingredients—no matter how trace in the final product—be listed on the label, meaning that Italian tomato products do not contain sugars or starches unless specifically listed on the label)

**HONEY** (preferably from a local source for the best flavor)

**DIJON MUSTARD** (with no starches or sugars added; try Woodstock Farms or Whole Foods brand)

**KOSHER SALT**

**SEA SALT** (Celtic, *fleur de sel,* gray, or Maldon flakes are the most flavorful)

**DRIED HERBS AND SPICES** including black peppercorns, paprika, ground cumin, ground oregano, turmeric, ground coriander, cinnamon, and cayenne (I like Spice Hunter, Whole Spice, Spice Garden, and Whole Foods brands. Beware of spice blends or mixes, which can have sugar as a hidden ingredient. Note: Those who have been on the diet for at least three months and are symptom-free can slowly add seeds and determine if tolerable.)

**VANILLA, ORANGE, ALMOND, MINT, AND LEMON EXTRACTS** (no additives)

**ALMOND FLOUR** (Already ground almond flour can be purchased from www.lucyskitchenshop.com. To make your own, process blanched almonds in a food processor until finely ground. Two cups whole almonds will make slightly less than 2 cups of ground. Almond flour can be stored in the freezer for up to four months.)

**ALL-NATURAL PEANUT BUTTER** (I like Marantha brand)

**ROASTED TAHINI** (sesame paste spread)

**WHOLE CASHEWS, PECANS, AND WALNUTS** (bought in bulk and stored in your freezer for up to four months)

**GROUND BLANCHED ALMONDS** (see Almond flour)

**MEDJOOL DATES** (loose, uncoated, and with no sugar added)

**RAISINS AND CURRANTS**

**GINGER**

**SCALLIONS**

**GARLIC**

**ONIONS**

**LEMONS**

**LIMES**

**ORGANIC DRIED RED LENTILS, SPLIT PEAS, WHITE NAVY BEANS, AND LITTLE FRENCH LENTILS**

**COCONUT MILK** (unsweetened and additive-free; The only one I have found without gums added is Trader Joe's Light Coconut Milk)

**UNFLAVORED GELATIN**

**BAKING SODA** (aluminum-free)


## REFRIGERATED ITEMS

**FARMER CHEESE** (dry-curd cottage cheese available at most supermarkets; I like Friendship Brand)

**ITALIAN PARMESAN CHEESE IN BLOCK FORM**

**BUTTER** (salted and unsalted)

**WHOLE MILK, HALF-AND-HALF, AND HEAVY CREAM** for yogurt making (Organic Valley brand has no gums in its products)

**EGGS**

**FRESH HERBS** including rosemary, thyme, mint, oregano, marjoram, tarragon, chives, chervil, cilantro, curry, and flat-leaf parsley (which you can keep in a glass of water in the fridge covered with a plastic bag to prolong storage)

**FRESH FRUITS AND VEGETABLES**

**NIÇOISE OLIVES** (no additives)


## FROZEN ITEMS

**RIPE BANANAS** (must have brown spots on them; store in the freezer for smoothies)

**FROZEN BLUEBERRIES, STRAWBERRIES, RASPBERRIES, SLICED PEACHES, AND PINEAPPLE CHUNKS**

# homemade yogurt

This yogurt is thick like Greek yogurt. It provides natural acidophilus, which helps your body rid itself of harmful bacteria and is also rich in calcium. Try to eat at least 1 cup (and no more than 3 cups) each day.

This yogurt is easy to make but must be properly prepared by letting it ferment for twenty-four hours. This allows enough time for the bacteria in the yogurt culture to break down the lactose (a disaccharide) in milk into galactose (a monosaccharide). I like Organic Valley brand milk and half-and-half, but any brand of milk with no added carrageenan is fine. You will need a yogurt maker to make it. I like the one by Yogourmet, available at Lucy's Kitchen Shop (see Resources, page 230). You can ask for a glass bucket insert, which I prefer instead of the standard plastic one, as it will be heated. For those sensitive to casein or cow's milk, goat's milk is a wonderful and very healthy option. Goat yogurt is watery, so you will need to drip it, following the instructions for Strained Yogurt (page 28).

**1 quart whole milk**
**1 quart half-and-half**
**2 packages (10 grams) Yogourmet starter**

Bring the milk and half-and-half to a simmer in a large saucepan over medium heat. Remove from the heat and allow to cool in the pan until lukewarm. Pour 1 cup of the liquid through a strainer into the inner bucket of the yogurt maker. Add the contents of the starter packets and whisk 20 times in both directions. Add the remaining milk mixture and whisk again 10 times each way. Put the top on the bucket, place the bucket in the outer container along with 1½ cups of water, and plug in the machine for 24 hours.

After 24 hours, do not open but place the inner container in the refrigerator for 8 hours more. The yogurt will keep, covered in the refrigerator, for up to 2 weeks.

## variations:

### EXTRA-RICH YOGURT
Substitute 1 quart half-and-half for the whole milk.

### CREAM YOGURT

Substitute 2 quarts heavy cream for the whole milk and half-and-half.

### LOW-FAT OR NONFAT YOGURT

Substitute 2 quarts reduced-fat or skim milk for the whole milk and half-and-half.

### STRAINED YOGURT

You can make extra-thick yogurt to use as a substitute for crème fraîche or sour cream, or to roll into balls and marinate with herbs and olive oil in the manner of fresh mozzarella bocconcini. Put some yogurt in a strainer lined with cheesecloth or an unbleached coffee filter. Set the strainer over a bowl and refrigerate for 30 minutes. Carefully pull up the corners of the cheesecloth and gently squeeze out any excess liquid. Discard the liquid. Two cups of yogurt will yield 1¾ cups of strained yogurt.

### HOMEMADE CRÈME FRAÎCHE

Make Strained Yogurt, above, using Extra-Rich Yogurt.

### YOGURT CHEESE

Put 2 quarts Homemade Yogurt in a large strainer lined with cheesecloth, paper towels, or an unbleached coffee filter. Set the strainer over a bowl and refrigerate until the yogurt is firm, at least 12 hours or, preferably, up to 3 days. Change the wet cheesecloth for a dry cheesecloth up to twice a day. Remove from the strainer, and discard the liquid in the bowl. The yogurt will keep for up to 1 week, covered, in the refrigerator. Makes about 1½ pounds.

### YOGURT-CHEESE BOCCONCINI

Using a melon baller, scoop Yogurt Cheese into balls and place in a medium container. Cover with olive oil and herbs, and marinate in the refrigerator for at least 3 hours or up to 1 week.

### YOGURT CHEESE CAPRESE SALAD

Slice the Yogurt Cheese into thick slices and place on a platter alternately with thick tomato slices and whole basil leaves. Sprinkle the platter with sea salt, freshly ground pepper, and a drizzle of olive oil.

## SNEAKY INGREDIENTS TO WATCH OUT FOR AND AVOID

These are some of the most common ingredients—found in packaged foods—that you need to avoid. They are not allowed on the diet because they are either multiple-chain sugars or starches that feed the bad bacteria in the gut. To find out more, go to www.breakingtheviciouscycle.info.

Carrageenan

Cellulose

FOS (fructooligosaccharides)

Kudzu, slippery elm, and arrowroot

Locust bean gum, guar gum, xantham gum, carrageenan

Maltodextrin

Pectin

Potato starch

Sorbitol, mannitol, and xylitol

Soy flour

Soy sauce

Sucrose, fructose, and evaporated cane juice

# appetizers, salads, and soups

Fresh Spring Rolls with Spicy Chile Dipping Sauce

Curried Deviled Eggs with Mango-Currant Chutney

Baked Brie and Garlic on Green Apple Slices

Skewered Shrimps in Mint Pesto

Roasted Vegetables with Lemon-Onion Dip

Vodka-and-Honey-Cured Salmon with Crème Fraîche

Celery Rémoulade

Fresh Shaved Beet Salad with Fresh Mint and Herbed Farmer
Cheese

Spinach Salad with Crispy Prosciutto, Poached Eggs,
and Caramelized Onions

Tabbouleh

Shaved Fennel, White Mushrooms, and Parmesan Salad

Salade Niçoise with Grilled Ahi

Thai Beef Salad with Papaya and Toasted Coconut

French Lentil Salad

Basic Chicken Stock

Roasted Vegetable Stock

French Three-Onion Soup with Gruyère

Italian White Bean Soup with Caramelized Fennel

Mexican Black Bean Soup

Egyptian Red Lentil Soup

Watercress and Cauliflower Puree with Parmesan Crackers

Tom Yum Kai with Coconut Milk and Lemongrass Infusion

Pistou with Pesto

Shiitake Cashew Soup

Hot and Sour Soup

Chilled Cucumber Soup with Yogurt and Dill

Chilled Pea Soup

Gazpacho

**the best thing about** all the first-course dishes in this chapter—besides the fact that they are delicious—is that your guests won't even realize these foods adhere to a special diet; instead, they'll be raving about the bright, clean flavors and wonderful taste that each dish has to offer. These favorite tried-and-true recipes are perfect for dinner parties, casual luncheons, and many other occasions. People following the SCD will no longer feel as if they're missing out when it comes to entertaining.

The appetizers and salads in this chapter range in variety from updated classics such as Curried Deviled Eggs with Mango-Currant Chutney (page 36) and Roasted Vegetables with Lemon-Onion Dip (page 40) to more elegant and exotic fare such as Fresh Spring Rolls with Spicy Chile Dipping Sauce (page 34) and Thai Beef Salad with Papaya and Toasted Coconut (page 52). Most of the salads can be served as main courses and are perfect accompaniments to the soups offered here.

For those on the Specific Carbohydrate Diet, soups are especially nourishing since they are so soothing and easy to digest. For those just starting the diet, soups should be the main fare until your body starts to feel better and you feel ready to move on to solid foods.

The soups offered in this chapter range from hot to cold, pureed to chunky, Thai to Mexican. Many of them start with a good solid stock such as Basic Chicken Stock (page 55) or Roasted Vegetable Stock (page 56), and then call for the freshest of seasonal ingredients. The higher the quality of ingredient you use, the better your food will taste. If you're in a pinch or short on time, you can use the store-bought stocks suggested in Stocking Your Kitchen (page 23).

Most of these soups would be equally appropriate and satisfying served as a main course for lunch or a light dinner or as a first course at dinner. Serve them as directed or try topping them with a variety of sauces or spreads, such as Spinach, Lemon, and Basil Pesto (page 75), Carrot-Ginger Paste (page 78), Lucques Olive Tapenade (page 87), or a splash of the best-quality extra-virgin olive oil you can find. Either way—presented simply or dressed up with a garnish—they are sure to be welcomed eagerly.

# fresh spring rolls with spicy chile dipping sauce

SERVES 8

These delectable hors d'oeuvres tend to disappear quickly. You won't miss the standard rice paper, which is replaced here with paper-thin slices of crisp, cool cucumber. If you are a vegetarian, simply omit the shrimp and increase the proportion of the other filling ingredients. If you prefer, you can substitute cooked and shredded chicken for the shrimp.

12 ounces medium peeled and deveined shrimp
One 3½-ounce package enoki mushrooms, ends trimmed
4 large cucumbers, peeled and ends trimmed
3 sprigs fresh mint leaves, sliced into thin ribbons
3 carrots, peeled and cut into thin matchsticks
1 mango, finely diced
1 avocado, finely diced
1 bunch fresh cilantro, roughly chopped
2 tablespoons freshly squeezed lemon juice (about 1 lemon)
Dipping Sauce (recipe follows)

Bring a medium saucepan of water to a boil. Add the shrimp, return to a boil, and cook for 1 minute. Use a slotted spoon to transfer the shrimp to a plate. Reserve the pan of boiling water. When the shrimp are cool enough to handle, cut them in half lengthwise. Set aside.

Cook the mushrooms for 3 minutes in the boiling water. Drain and set aside to cool.

Using a mandoline or a sharp knife, thinly slice the cucumbers lengthwise. Stop when you reach the seed core and give each cucumber a quarter turn before repeating. Lay 3 or 4 slices at a time on a flat work surface, overlapping them to form a rectangular sheet. You should be able to make about 8 sheets. Lay 2 to 3 shrimp halves on each cucumber sheet. Scatter ribbons of mint on each sheet. Scatter the carrots, mango, avocado, enoki mushrooms, and cilantro on each sheet and sprinkle a little lemon juice on top.

Roll tightly lengthwise. Cut each roll crosswise into 2 or 3 sections. Standing them up on their ends, arrange the rolls on a platter. Prepare the Dipping Sauce and place the bowl in the middle of the platter. This can be made several hours in advance and refrigerated.

# DIPPING SAUCE

¼ **cup toasted sesame oil**
¼ **cup freshly squeezed lime juice (2 to 3 limes)**
**2 tablespoons white wine vinegar or brown rice vinegar**
**3 tablespoons honey**
¼ **cup plain unsalted peanuts**
**1 fresh red or green hot chile, seeded and sliced**
**1 clove garlic**
**One 1-inch knob fresh ginger, peeled**
**1 teaspoon salt**

Combine the sesame oil, lime juice, vinegar, honey, peanuts, chile, garlic, ginger, and salt in a blender and puree until smooth. This can be prepared 1 day in advance and kept in the refrigerator.

# curried deviled eggs with mango-currant chutney

These deviled eggs are an updated version of my mother's fabulous original recipe. The mango-currant chutney adds a wonderful dimension of flavor.

**12 hard-boiled eggs, peeled and halved lengthwise**
**1 cup Aïoli (page 82)**
**1 tablespoon mustard powder**
**2 tablespoons curry powder**
**2 tablespoons paprika, plus extra for garnish**
**½ tablespoon celery salt**
**1 tablespoon freshly cracked pepper**
**1 tablespoon snipped fresh chives**
**1 tablespoon finely chopped flat-leaf parsley**
**½ cup Mango-Currant Chutney (recipe follows)**

Separate the yolks from the whites of the eggs, placing the yolks in a medium bowl and reserving the whites on a platter for later. Combine the egg yolks, Aïoli, mustard powder, curry, paprika, celery salt, pepper, chives, and parsley. Using a fork, mash everything together and mix well. Spoon the mixture into the egg white halves.

Prepare the chutney. Place ½ teaspoon of chutney on top of each egg half and garnish with a sprinkle of paprika.

# MANGO-CURRANT CHUTNEY

MAKES ABOUT 2 CUPS

**2 mangoes, peeled, seeded, and diced**
**¼ cup currants**
**¼ cup chopped Medjool dates**
**1 tablespoon grated fresh ginger**
**½ teaspoon minced jalapeño pepper**
**1 clove garlic, minced**
**½ cup apple cider vinegar**
**¼ cup honey**
**Pinch of salt and freshly ground pepper**

In a medium saucepan, combine the mangoes, currants, dates, ginger, jalapeño, garlic, vinegar, and honey and season with salt and pepper. Bring to a boil over high heat, then lower the heat and simmer, stirring frequently, until thick, about 30 minutes. Set aside to cool and then refrigerate until cold, at least 30 minutes or up to 3 days.

# baked brie and garlic on green apple slices

SERVES A CROWD (20 TO 25 PEOPLE)

This is a great dish to serve at a cocktail party. Guests will love spreading the sweet baked garlic on a fresh crunchy apple slice and then topping it with gooey baked brie. Delicious!

**2 tablespoons extra-virgin olive oil**
**30 cloves garlic, peeled**
**½ wheel Brie cheese (1½ to 2 pounds)**
**12 green apples, cored**
**½ lemon**
**Parsley sprigs for garnish**

Preheat the oven to 400° F.

In an 8-inch baking pan, mix the oil and garlic. Cover with foil and place in the oven for 45 to 60 minutes, until the garlic is golden brown and very soft.

After 40 minutes, put the Brie in a shallow baking dish and place it in the oven for 15 to 20 minutes, until the cheese is slightly drippy.

While the Brie is baking, cut the apples into thin wedges. Put them in a bowl, squeeze the juice from the lemon on top, and gently toss to coat the apples. Set aside.

Remove the garlic and Brie from the oven and set the Brie on a serving platter. Mash the garlic with the oil to form a paste and place in a small serving bowl next to the Brie. Fan out the apple wedges and place on the platter around the Brie. Garnish with parsley and serve with several cheese knives on the side.

# skewered shrimps in mint pesto

SERVES 6 AS AN APPETIZER

The fresh, bright taste of mint stands up to the grilled shrimp here and is a welcome alternative to typical basil pesto. Try this pesto with grilled chicken as well.

½ **cup olive oil**
**5 cloves garlic**
**2 cups fresh mint leaves**
**1 tablespoon grated lemon zest**
**Salt and freshly ground pepper to taste**
**1 pound peeled and deveined medium shrimp (tails left on)**
**About 12 bamboo skewers**
½ **cup freshly squeezed lemon juice (2 to 3 lemons)**

In a food processor or blender, combine the oil, garlic, mint, zest, salt, and pepper, and blend well. Pour half of this mint pesto into a wide, shallow dish. Reserve the remaining pesto in a pretty serving bowl, cover, and refrigerate until needed. Add the shrimp to the pesto in the dish and turn to coat. Refrigerate for at least 1 hour or overnight.

Soak the bamboo skewers in water for 30 minutes. Preheat a grill to medium-high.

Place the shrimp on the skewers (about 2 on each) and grill for 2 minutes per side, until pink and just cooked through.

Serve hot with a drizzle of lemon juice and reserved pesto.

# roasted vegetables with lemon-onion dip

SERVES 12

This colorful and bountiful presentation will be the focal point of any party table. Roasting provides the vegetables with extra sweetness, which is nicely complemented by the tangy dip.

**VEGETABLES**

1 pound baby beets, peeled, with a bit of stem left on

3 tablespoons olive oil

Salt and freshly ground pepper

1 pound baby carrots, peeled, preferably with a bit of stem left on

1 pound fat asparagus spears

4 medium zucchini, split lengthwise into quarters

**DIP**

1¾ cups Strained Yogurt (page 28)

½ teaspoon celery salt

Pinch of freshly ground pepper

½ cup freshly squeezed lemon juice (2 to 3 lemons)

3 tablespoons dried onion chips

**TO PREPARE THE VEGETABLES**

Preheat the oven to 425°F.

Put the beets in a roasting pan. Drizzle with 1 tablespoon oil, sprinkle with salt and pepper, and mix well. Roast, tossing occasionally to prevent burning, for about 30 minutes, until tender. Transfer to a plate and cool to room temperature.

Wash and dry the roasting pan. Toss the carrots in the pan with 1 tablespoon oil and roast for 5 minutes. Add the asparagus to the pan along with the remaining tablespoon oil and toss to combine. Roast for 15 minutes, then add the zucchini and gently toss with the other vegetables. Roast for 10 to 15 minutes, until the carrots are golden brown and all the vegetables are tender. Remove from the oven and season with salt and pepper. Cool to room temperature.

### TO PREPARE THE DIP

Put the strained yogurt in a small serving bowl. Add the celery salt, pepper, juice, and onion chips, and mix well. (The dip can be made 2 days in advance and refrigerated until serving.)

### TO SERVE

Set the bowl of dip in the middle of a large serving platter and fan out the beets, carrots, asparagus, and zucchini around it like the petals of a flower.

# vodka-and-honey-cured salmon with crème fraîche

MAKES 35 TO 40 THIN SLICES

I love cured salmon, but all the premade ones seem to add sugar during the curing process. I prefer to cure my own salmon using honey instead of sugar. It's incredibly easy to do this at home; the salmon simply sits in its marinade in the fridge for 2 days. Serve with Buttery Herb and Garlic Crackers (page 159) or on toasted Macadamia Medjool Date Cake (page 177) with Homemade Crème Fraîche (page 28).

**One 2-pound wild salmon fillet (the thinner the better), skin and bones removed, rinsed and dried**

**½ cup kosher salt**

**¼ cup honey**

**¼ cup vodka**

**2 tablespoons grated orange zest**

**2 tablespoons grated lemon zest**

**2 tablespoons crushed green peppercorns**

**¼ cup fresh dill**

**Chopped red onion, Homemade Crème Fraîche (page 28), capers, lemon wedges, or chopped parsley for garnish (optional)**

Lay the salmon on a long sheet of plastic wrap.

Mix the salt, honey, vodka, zests, peppercorns, and dill in a medium bowl. Spread the mixture all over the fish and press it into the flesh.

Cover the salmon well with plastic wrap and set it in a shallow baking dish that is long enough to lay the salmon flat. Place another long dish or cookie sheet on top of the salmon and add a couple of heavy cans to the dish to weigh it down. Leave in the refrigerator for 2 days.

Slice the salmon thinly and serve with your favorite garnish.

# celery rémoulade

SERVES 6 TO 8

This is a classic tangy and creamy French salad that is reminiscent of coleslaw but made with earthy celery root instead. This recipe is intended for those who have been on the SCD diet for at least three months and are symptom-free.

½ cup freshly squeezed lemon juice (2 to 3 lemons)

Salt and freshly ground pepper

½ cup Strained Yogurt (page 28)

¼ cup Homemade Dijon Mustard (page 80)

¼ cup Aïoli (page 82)

1 large celery root, peeled and grated (about 4 cups)

2 tablespoons drained capers

¼ cup finely chopped flat-leaf parsley

In a large bowl, whisk the juice with a pinch each of salt and black pepper. Whisk in the yogurt, mustard, and Aïoli. Add the celery root and capers, and mix well to coat. Adjust the seasoning with additional salt and pepper if necessary. Serve on a platter with the parsley scattered on top.

### curried celery rémoulade:

Add 1 tablespoon curry powder (no starches added) to the lemon juice. Toss in ½ cup currants at the end.

# fresh shaved beet salad with fresh mint and herbed farmer cheese

SERVES 6

This lovely summer salad not only tastes wonderful but is beautiful to behold with its multicolored beets flecked with mint and topped with crumbled cheese. For those who just started the diet or are not quite ready for raw vegetables, steam the beets slightly for a few minutes.

Farmer cheese, also known as dry-curd cottage cheese or hoop cheese, is a great substitute for cottage cheese, ricotta, feta, cream cheese, and chèvre, which all contain lactose and are therefore not allowed on the diet. Farmer cheese can be found in most supermarkets. Use as is or infuse it with flavor, such as in this dish where it is mixed with truffle oil and fresh herbs.

6 medium beets, preferably in assorted colors, peeled
1 small bunch fresh mint leaves, cut into thin ribbons
1 clove garlic, minced
6 tablespoons extra-virgin olive oil
¼ cup freshly squeezed lemon juice (about 1 lemon)
2 tablespoons freshly squeezed orange juice
Salt and freshly ground pepper to taste
½ cup Herbed Farmer Cheese (recipe follows)

Using a mandoline or a very sharp knife, slice the beets paper thin. Put them in a medium serving bowl. Add the mint, garlic, oil, and juices, and mix well. Add salt and pepper, and top with the farmer cheese.

# HERBED FARMER CHEESE

**MAKES ½ CUP**

½ cup farmer cheese
2 tablespoons white truffle oil (optional)
2 tablespoons freshly squeezed lemon juice
1 teaspoon minced garlic
2 teaspoons chopped fresh thyme
2 teaspoons chopped fresh parsley
2 teaspoons chopped fresh tarragon
Pinch of salt

Mix together with a fork the cheese, truffle oil, lemon juice, garlic, thyme, parsley, tarragon, and salt and mash until well blended. This will keep for 3 days in the refrigerator.

# spinach salad with crispy prosciutto, poached eggs, and caramelized onions

SERVES 4

This hearty bistro salad is healthy, indulgent, and utterly satisfying when accompanied by a glass of dry white wine.

1 teaspoon plus 1 tablespoon olive oil

1 tablespoon unsalted butter

1 large red onion, thinly sliced

1 tablespoon honey

4 ounces thinly sliced Italian prosciutto, cut into 1- to 2-inch pieces

6 cups fresh spinach

¼ cup French Vinaigrette (recipe follows)

4 large eggs, poached (see box)

Salt and freshly ground pepper to taste

In a sauté pan, heat 1 teaspoon oil and the butter over medium heat. Add the onion and cook for 4 minutes, until translucent. Add the honey and cook over medium-low heat until golden brown, about 1 more minute. Remove from the pan and transfer to a plate to cool.

Heat the remaining tablespoon of oil in the same pan over high heat and add the prosciutto pieces. Cook for about 1 minute, then turn and cook until the other side is crispy and curly, about 4 minutes. Remove to paper towels to drain.

Place the spinach in a large salad bowl. Add the onion and prosciutto. Dress with the vinaigrette, toss well, and divide among 4 plates. Place a poached egg on top of each serving. Sprinkle with salt and pepper.

# FRENCH VINAIGRETTE

MAKES ¾ CUP

2 tablespoons minced shallots
1 tablespoon Homemade Dijon Mustard (page 80)
¼ cup red wine vinegar
Salt and freshly ground pepper to taste
½ cup extra-virgin olive oil

In a large measuring cup (which is easy to pour), whisk the shallots, mustard, vinegar, salt, and pepper. Keep whisking and slowly drizzle in the oil until well mixed. This can be made up to 2 days in advance and kept in the refrigerator.

## POACHED EGGS

Boil 8 cups water in a saucepan and add a pinch of salt and 1 tablespoon white vinegar. Crack 1 egg into a small bowl. Slide the egg gently into the pan and boil for 2 minutes or to desired doneness, skimming off any foam. With a slotted spoon, transfer the egg to a paper towel to drain. Repeat with the remaining eggs.

# tabbouleh

Chopped zucchini replaces the traditional bulgur wheat in this flavorful salad that is loaded with fresh herbs. Serve with White Bean Hummus (page 84), Kibbeh with Yogurt and Mint (page 122), and Cucumber Raita (page 88) as a Middle Eastern platter. Top it all off with Persimmon Cream Cups (page 180) for dessert.

5 medium zucchini, peeled
1 large bunch fresh flat-leaf parsley, leaves only
1 large bunch fresh mint, leaves only
3 large tomatoes, peeled, seeded, and chopped
7 scallions, white and green parts, thinly sliced
¼ cup freshly squeezed lemon juice (about 1 lemon)
1 medium shallot, minced
1 clove garlic, minced
¼ cup extra-virgin olive oil
Salt and freshly ground pepper to taste

In a food processor, pulse the zucchini until they become very small, like couscous. Transfer to a large bowl. Chop the parsley and mint leaves in the food processor and add to the zucchini. Stir in the tomatoes and scallions.

   In a small bowl, mix the juice, shallot, garlic, and oil, and pour on the vegetables. Mix well and chill for at least 30 minutes or up to 4 hours. Season with salt and pepper before serving.

# shaved fennel, white mushrooms, and parmesan salad

SERVES 6 TO 8

Each of the ingredients in this dish has a distinct flavor of its own, and they combine wonderfully in this beautiful pale green, yellow, and white salad. Serve with Whole Roasted Red Snapper Stuffed with Fennel and Citrus (page 95).

- 12 ounces (4 cups) white or cremini mushrooms, stemmed and caps cleaned
- 1 large bulb fennel, a few fronds reserved
- 6 spears Belgian endive, cut into ½-inch slices
- ½ cup shaved Parmesan cheese (use a vegetable peeler or a mandoline)
- ½ cup freshly squeezed lemon juice (2 to 3 lemons)
- ½ cup extra-virgin olive oil
- Salt and freshly ground pepper to taste

Thinly slice the mushrooms with a mandoline or a sharp knife and place in a salad bowl. Shave the fennel and add to the mushrooms along with the endive and Parmesan.

In a small bowl, whisk the lemon juice, oil, salt, and pepper. Pour over the salad and gently toss. Garnish with the reserved fennel fronds.

# salade niçoise with grilled ahi

SERVES 6 TO 8

This is the perfect dish for a summer luncheon. Make sure to buy very fresh sushi-grade raw tuna or use high-quality canned tuna packed in water. If you miss the taste and texture of potatoes in a traditional Salad Niçoise, try substituting blanched cauliflower or butternut squash.

### VINAIGRETTE

2 tablespoons minced shallot

1 tablespoon Homemade Dijon Mustard (page 80)

¼ cup red wine vinegar

Salt and freshly ground pepper to taste

½ cup extra-virgin olive oil

### SALAD

8 ounces French green beans, stemmed

2 pounds fresh sushi-quality Ahi tuna steaks, about 1 inch thick

Salt and freshly ground pepper

4 heads romaine lettuce, leaves separated

6 hard-boiled eggs, peeled and quartered

1 cup fresh Niçoise olives

¼ cup drained capers

½ pint cherry tomatoes, sliced in half

¼ cup chopped fresh cilantro

¼ cup roughly chopped fresh flat-leaf parsley

2 tablespoons chopped fresh tarragon

2 lemons, quartered

## TO PREPARE THE VINAIGRETTE

In a small bowl, whisk together the shallot, mustard, vinegar, salt, and pepper. Slowly drizzle in the oil while whisking so the dressing emulsifies. This can be made 1 day in advance and kept in the refrigerator.

## TO PREPARE THE SALAD

Bring a medium saucepan of salted water to a boil. Fill a medium bowl halfway with ice and cover with cold water. Add the green beans to the pan and boil for 1 minute. Drain and transfer to the ice bath to cool. Drain well and set aside or cover and refrigerate overnight.

Preheat the grill to high.

Season the tuna with salt and pepper. Grill the tuna for 2 to 3 minutes per side for medium rare. Set aside.

Fan out the romaine leaves on a large platter like the petals of a flower or arrange on 6 or 8 plates. Arrange the beans in bundles evenly around the romaine leaves. Place the eggs, olives, capers, and tomatoes decoratively on the platter. Slice and fan out the tuna in the middle of the platter. Sprinkle the cilantro, parsley, and tarragon on top, and then drizzle with the vinaigrette. Set the lemon wedges around the platter before serving.

# thai beef salad with papaya and toasted coconut

SERVES 4

This delicious Asian salad, featuring traditional Thai flavors of ginger, chile, lime, and coconut, can be served as a first course or as an entrée.

### DRESSING

¼ cup freshly squeezed lemon juice (about 1 lemon)

2 tablespoons freshly squeezed lime juice

2 tablespoons freshly squeezed orange juice

2 tablespoons toasted sesame oil

1 small clove garlic, minced

1 tablespoon grated fresh ginger

1 green or red chile, seeded and sliced into thin strips

1 tablespoon black sesame seeds (if tolerated), toasted

1 tablespoon date paste or 2 Medjool dates, mashed

1 teaspoon cayenne pepper

Salt and freshly ground pepper to taste

### SALAD

1 pound steak, such as filet mignon, New York strip, ribeye, or flank

Salt and freshly ground pepper to taste

2 cups shredded purple cabbage (1 small head)

8 to 10 scallions, sliced on the diagonal

1 small red onion, very thinly sliced

2 medium carrots, peeled and cut into matchsticks

2 red bell peppers, peeled, seeded, and cut into matchsticks

1 ripe papaya, cut into matchsticks

1 medium cucumber, peeled, seeded, and cut into matchsticks

1 cup chopped fresh cilantro

½ cup thinly sliced fresh mint leaves

½ cup dried unsweetened coconut, toasted (see box)

2 Kaffir lime leaves, finely shredded, or grated zest of 1 lime

½ cup cashews, toasted (see box)

## TO PREPARE THE DRESSING

In a small bowl, stir together the lemon, lime, and orange juice, sesame oil, garlic, ginger, chile, sesame seeds, date paste, cayenne, salt, and pepper. Set aside for 1 hour to allow the flavors to blend, then cover and refrigerate.

## TO PREPARE THE SALAD

Preheat a grill to high.

Season the steak with salt and pepper and grill for 7 to 9 minutes on each side for medium rare. Transfer to a cutting board and let rest for at least 5 minutes. (This can be done 1 hour ahead.)

Scatter the cabbage, scallions, onions, carrots, bell peppers, papaya, and cucumber on a large serving platter. Slice the steak on the diagonal, against the grain, as thinly as you can. Fan out the slices on top of the vegetables. Sprinkle with the cilantro, mint, coconut, lime, and cashews. Drizzle the dressing over all and season with salt and pepper before serving.

### TOASTED COCONUT

Preheat the oven to 375°F.

Place shredded or shaved coconut on a cookie sheet and toast in the oven for 8 to 10 minutes, or until golden brown. Turn once or twice with a spatula to prevent the coconut from burning. Remove the baking sheet from the oven and allow the coconut to cool. Store in an airtight container for up to 3 weeks.

### TOASTED NUTS

Preheat the oven to 375°F.

Place the nuts on a cookie sheet and toast in the oven for 5 to 10 minutes, until golden brown. Turn once or twice with a spatula to prevent the nuts from burning. Remove the baking sheet from the oven and allow the nuts to cool. Store in an airtight container for up to 3 weeks.

### PAN-TOASTED SEEDS OR WHOLE SPICES

Place the seeds in a small sauté pan over medium heat. Stir often with a wooden spoon until the seeds or spices are lightly toasted and fragrant, about 3 to 6 minutes. Once cool, the seeds can be stored in an airtight container for up to 3 weeks.

# french lentil salad

Grapefruit juice, sweet currants, and cumin lend exotic and unexpected bursts of flavor to this delicious salad.

**2 cups French green lentils**
**½ cup extra-virgin olive oil**
**¼ cup freshly squeezed lemon juice (about 1 lemon)**
**¼ cup freshly squeezed grapefruit juice (1 small grapefruit)**
**2 tablespoons ground cumin**
**1 tablespoon celery salt**
**2 teaspoons curry powder**
**1 teaspoon ground coriander**
**½ teaspoon cayenne pepper**
**3 large shallots, finely chopped**
**3 cloves garlic, minced**
**2 tablespoons fresh thyme**
**1 tablespoon freshly grated lemon zest**
**½ cup currants**
**1 fennel bulb, very thinly sliced**
**4 stalks celery, finely chopped**
**1 cup chopped fresh parsley**
**½ cup chopped fresh cilantro**
**Salt and freshly ground pepper to taste**

Rinse and pick over the lentils to remove any small pebbles, and then soak in water for 24 hours, changing the water halfway through. Rinse and drain.

Place the lentils in a large saucepan and add enough water to cover them generously, about 6 cups. Bring to a boil, then lower the heat and simmer for 20 to 25 minutes, until tender. Drain well and set aside.

In a large bowl, whisk together the oil, juices, cumin, celery salt, curry powder, coriander, cayenne, shallots, garlic, thyme, and zest. Add the lentils, currants, fennel, celery, parsley, and cilantro. Season with salt and pepper. Mix well. Serve warm or chilled. This can be made 1 day in advance.

# basic chicken stock

MAKES ABOUT 3 QUARTS

This is the most important recipe when you are beginning the SCD or having an intestinal flare-up. This soup puts you back on track and lets the healing begin. The lemon juice helps extract all the minerals from the chicken bones and provides a rich flavor. You can cook the stock down if you want a more concentrated broth; simply boil, uncovered, until the soup reduces to half its original volume.

3 to 4 pounds chicken parts, such as bone-in thighs, wings, legs, backs, and necks

3 medium yellow onions, cut into quarters

1 head garlic, cut in half crosswise

3 medium carrots, cut into 3 pieces

3 stalks celery, cut into 3 pieces

1 medium bulb fennel, cut into quarters

2 bay leaves

¼ cup freshly squeezed lemon juice (about 1 lemon)

1 teaspoon freshly ground pepper

Place all the ingredients in a large stockpot and add enough cold water to cover (about 4 quarts). Bring to a boil over high heat, then reduce the heat to low and simmer for 4 hours. Skim off any foam on the surface of the stock as it cooks.

Strain the stock through a fine-mesh strainer into a big pot. The stock can be used immediately. To store it, allow it to come to room temperature and then refrigerate. Once the stock has chilled, you can scrape off the layer of fat from the top and discard. The stock can be kept in the refrigerator for up to 1 week or frozen for up to 3 months.

# roasted vegetable stock

MAKES ABOUT 3 QUARTS

This delicious stock is wonderful on its own or as a base for other soups, vegetarian or otherwise.

3 cups mushroom stems, wiped clean (about 8 ounces mushrooms; save the caps for another use)

2 medium leeks, white and green part, roughly chopped and thoroughly cleaned

2 medium yellow onions, roughly chopped

1 small zucchini, roughly chopped

1 medium carrot, roughly chopped

1 stalk celery, roughly chopped

12 cloves garlic, roughly chopped

2 tablespoons olive oil

Salt and pepper to taste

½ cup fresh parsley

2 tablespoons fresh thyme

2 tablespoons fresh marjoram (optional)

2 bay leaves

1 cup white wine

Preheat the oven to 450° F.

In a large roasting pan, combine the mushroom stems, leeks, onions, zucchini, carrot, celery, and garlic. Add the oil, salt, and pepper, and mix until all the vegetables are well coated. Roast for about 40 minutes, stirring occasionally, until the vegetables are browned.

Transfer the vegetables to a large soup pot and add cold water to cover (about 3 quarts). Add the parsley, thyme, marjoram, and bay leaves, and bring to a boil over high heat. Skim the surface to remove any foam. Lower the heat, stir in the wine, and simmer for 30 minutes.

Strain the stock through a fine-mesh strainer. The stock can be used immediately. To store it, cool to room temperature and refrigerate for up to 1 week or freeze for up to 3 months.

## french three-onion soup with gruyère

SERVES 8

This recipe is reminiscent of the classic French onion soup minus the starch. Rich, flavorful, and satisfying, this is the perfect homemade soup for a cold day. Serve with your favorite homemade crackers or toasted nut bread.

**4 medium yellow onions, thickly sliced**

**2 tablespoons olive oil**

**Salt and freshly ground pepper to taste**

**3 large leeks, white and green parts, sliced and thoroughly cleaned**

**6 shallots, sliced**

**8 cloves garlic, sliced**

**¼ cup white wine**

**8 cups Basic Chicken Stock (page 55) or Roasted Vegetable Stock
    (page 56)**

**8 ounces Gruyère cheese, grated (2 cups)**

In a big soup pot over medium heat, sauté the onions in the oil for 20 minutes. Add the salt and pepper and then the leeks, shallots, and garlic. Stir before pouring in the wine. Cook for 1 minute. Stir in the stock and bring to a boil. Lower the heat and simmer, covered, for 30 minutes. (The soup can be refrigerated for up to 3 days or frozen for 1 month at this point. Return to a boil before proceeding.)

Preheat the broiler.

Ladle the soup into ovenproof bowls and cover each serving with a generous dusting of Gruyère. Put the bowls on a cookie sheet and place under the broiler for 1 minute, or until the cheese bubbles. Serve immediately.

# italian white bean soup with caramelized fennel

It is important to soak the beans for this hearty soup in water for twenty-four hours to remove excess starch. You should be on the diet a minimum of three months or completely symptom free before introducing beans into your diet.

**4 cups dried white navy beans**
**3 tablespoons olive oil**
**3 medium yellow onions, roughly chopped**
**12 cloves garlic, roughly chopped**
**3 medium bulbs fennel, sliced (save the green fronds for garnish)**
**1 tablespoon unsalted butter**
**1 tablespoon fresh marjoram**
**1 tablespoon fresh thyme**
**Salt**
**2 tablespoons dry white wine**
**Freshly ground pepper**
**White truffle oil for garnish (optional)**

Rinse and pick over the beans to remove any small pebbles, and then soak in water for 24 hours, changing the water halfway through. Rinse and drain.

Heat 2 tablespoons olive oil in a large soup pot over medium heat. Add the onions and sauté until translucent, about 5 minutes. Add the garlic and cook 1 more minute. Strain the beans and add them to the pot along with 8 cups water to cover. Bring to a boil, skimming off any scum. Lower the heat, cover the pot, and simmer the beans for about 2 hours, until they are soft. (Do not add salt at this point, because this will toughen the beans.)

While the beans are cooking, heat a skillet over high heat and add the remaining table-spoon of olive oil. Add the fennel and cook for 1 minute. Lower the heat to medium-low and add the butter, marjoram, thyme, and a pinch of salt. Cook, covered, until golden brown, about 15 minutes. Uncover, add the wine, and cook for 1 minute. Remove from the heat.

In a blender or food processor, puree the beans and their cooking liquid with the fennel in batches. (The soup can be refrigerated for up to 1 week or frozen for up to 3 months.)

Place the soup in a large pot and bring to a simmer. Season to taste with salt and pepper. Divide among soup bowls and garnish with a sprig of fennel and truffle oil if desired.

# mexican black bean soup

SERVES 8 TO 10

Black beans are allowed on the SCD when you are symptom-free. The soaking process helps remove excess starch and makes the beans more digestible. This filling and flavorful soup is a nourishing and delicious way to introduce black beans into your diet.

8 cups dried black beans

2 tablespoons olive oil

3 medium yellow onions, finely chopped

2 medium carrots, finely chopped

2 stalks celery, finely chopped

10 cloves garlic, minced

1 green jalapeño pepper, seeded and minced

3 tablespoons ground cumin

1 tablespoon dried oregano

1 teaspoon cayenne pepper

1 bay leaf

Salt and freshly ground pepper to taste

Crumbled hoop cheese, Monterey Jack cheese, or Manchego cheese, crème fraîche, salsa, chopped cilantro, or crumbled bacon for garnish (optional)

Rinse and pick over the beans to remove any small pebbles, and then soak in water for 24 hours, changing the water halfway through. Rinse and drain.

In a large soup pot, heat the oil over medium-high heat. Add the onions and sauté until translucent, about 5 minutes. Add the carrots and celery, and cook a few more minutes. Add the garlic, jalapeño, cumin, oregano, cayenne, and bay leaf, and cook for 2 more minutes. Add the beans and 10 cups water to cover. (Do not add salt at this point because it will toughen the beans.) Stir well, cover, and bring to a boil. Lower the heat and simmer, covered, for about 1 hour, until the beans are soft. Discard the bay leaf.

In a blender or food processor, puree the beans and their liquid in small batches to the desired smoothness. If the soup seems too thick, thin it with a little water. (At this point the soup can be refrigerated for up to 1 week or frozen for up to 3 months.)

Season with salt and pepper, and serve in warmed bowls with your favorite garnish.

# egyptian red lentil soup

This fragrant soup, rich with spices, is for those who have been on the diet for at least a few months and are symptom-free. Serve with Shaved Fennel, White Mushrooms, and Parmesan Salad (page 49).

**4 cups dried red lentils**
**2 tablespoons olive oil, plus extra for serving**
**2 large yellow onions, diced**
**8 cloves garlic, minced**
**2 tablespoons ground cumin**
**1 tablespoon dried oregano**
**1 tablespoon paprika**
**2 tablespoons tomato paste**
**Salt and freshly ground pepper to taste**
**½ lemon for garnish**
**Snipped fresh chives for garnish (optional)**

Rinse and pick over the lentils to remove any small pebbles, and then soak in water for 24 hours, changing the water halfway through. Rinse and drain.

In a large soup pot, heat the oil over medium heat. Add the onions and sauté until translucent, about 5 minutes. Add the garlic, cumin, oregano, and paprika, and cook for 2 more minutes. Add the lentils and 8 cups water and stir well, scraping the bottom of the pot to prevent the lentils from sticking. Add the tomato paste and stir thoroughly again. Cover and bring to a boil, then lower the heat and simmer, covered, until the lentils are broken up, about 1½ hours.

Season with salt and pepper and stir again. (At this point the soup can be refrigerated for up to 1 week or frozen for up to 3 months.)

Serve in big bowls with a squirt of fresh lemon juice, a drizzle of oil, and some chives.

# watercress and cauliflower puree with parmesan crackers

SERVES 4

This is a lovely *potage,* or thick pureed soup, perfect for winter. Cauliflower is a great substitute for the standard potato thickener.

1 tablespoon olive oil
1 medium yellow onion, chopped
1 small cauliflower, roughly chopped
4 cups Basic Chicken Stock (page 55) or Roasted Vegetable Stock
   (page 56) or Pacific Foods Organic Vegetable Stock
4 tablespoons unsalted butter
Salt and freshly ground pepper to taste
2 bunches watercress, stems removed
Parmesan Crackers (recipe follows)

Heat the oil in a large soup pot over medium-high heat. Add the onion and cook until translucent, about 5 minutes. Add the cauliflower and cook for 2 minutes. Pour in the stock, bring to a boil, cover, lower the heat, and simmer for about 10 minutes, until the cauliflower is soft. Add the butter and season with salt and pepper. Add the watercress and remove from the heat. When the mixture has cooled somewhat, place in a blender or a food processor in batches and process until smooth. (The soup can be refrigerated for up to 3 days or frozen for 1 month at this point.) Reheat if necessary. Ladle into bowls and top with a couple of Parmesan crackers.

## PARMESAN CRACKERS

MAKES EIGHT 2-INCH CRACKERS

1 cup freshly grated Parmesan cheese

Preheat the oven to 375°F.
   Place a piece of uncoated parchment paper on a cookie sheet. Place tablespoons of Parmesan, evenly spaced and 1 inch apart, all over the cookie sheet. Bake for 15 minutes, until golden brown. Allow to cool completely. Store in an airtight container for up to 5 days.

# tom yum kai with coconut milk and lemongrass infusion

SERVES 4

The combination of coconut, lemongrass, and Asian curry forms the perfect balance of sweet, sour, and heat in this exotic Thai soup.

2 tablespoons peanut oil

8 ounces boneless, skinless chicken breast, cut into very thin strips

1 medium leek, white and green parts, cut into matchsticks and thoroughly cleaned

2 cups Infused Basic Chicken Stock (recipe follows)

One 14-ounce can unsweetened coconut milk

3 Kaffir lime leaves or 1 tablespoon grated lime zest

1 dried lemon or lime (can be found in specialty shops), smashed to release flavor (optional)

1 to 2 Thai chiles to taste, seeded, stemmed, and minced

1 small bunch cilantro, chopped, plus extra whole leaves for garnish

¼ cup freshly squeezed lime juice (2 to 3 limes)

In a soup pot, heat 1 tablespoon peanut oil over medium-high heat. Add the chicken and cook until golden brown, stirring as needed, about 10 minutes. Transfer the chicken to a plate and set aside.

Add the remaining tablespoon of oil to the pan along with the leek. Sauté until the leek is translucent, about 4 minutes. Add the stock infusion, coconut milk, lime leaves, dried lime, and chile. Bring to a boil.

Return the chicken to the pot, cover, lower the heat, and simmer for about 5 minutes. Stir in the cilantro and lime juice. (At this point the soup can be refrigerated for up to 3 days or frozen for 1 month.) Ladle into warmed bowls and top with whole cilantro leaves.

# INFUSED BASIC CHICKEN STOCK

MAKES 2 CUPS

2½ cups Basic Chicken Stock (page 55)
1 stalk lemongrass, roughly chopped
½ Thai bird chile
2 sprigs Thai basil

Combine all the ingredients in a saucepan and bring to a boil over high heat. Boil for 1 to 2 minutes to reduce to 2 cups. Strain.

# pistou with pesto

SERVES 8 TO 10

A savory soup from the south of France, this is especially delicious in late summer and early fall when all these vegetables are at their peak of flavor. Try adding a poached egg on top for a rich treat.

2 tablespoons olive oil

2 medium onions, diced

2 large leeks, white and green parts, sliced and thoroughly cleaned

2 cloves garlic, minced

8 cups Basic Chicken Stock (page 55) or Roasted Vegetable Stock
   (page 56)

4 medium tomatoes, seeded and chopped

1 large fennel bulb, sliced

2 medium carrots, sliced

2 stalks celery, sliced

4 medium zucchini, sliced

3 ounces green beans, cut into ½-inch pieces

½ cup sliced Swiss chard

Salt and freshly ground pepper to taste

1 cup Spinach, Lemon, and Basil Pesto (page 75)

Freshly grated Parmesan for serving

In a large soup pot, heat the oil over medium heat. Add the onions and sauté until translucent, about 5 minutes. Add the leeks and cook for 2 more minutes. Add the garlic and cook for 1 more minute. Pour in the stock and add the tomatoes, fennel, carrots, celery, zucchini, green beans, and Swiss chard. Bring to a boil, cover, lower the heat, and simmer for 20 minutes, until the vegetables are very tender. Add the salt and pepper. (At this point the soup can be refrigerated for up to 3 days or frozen for 1 month.) Serve in big warmed bowls with a dollop of pesto and some freshly grated Parmesan cheese.

# shiitake cashew soup

SERVES 6 TO 8

This tangy Asian soup gets its creamy consistency from soaked and pureed cashews.

1 cup cashews, plus extra cashews halved for garnish

1 tablespoon olive oil

2 medium yellow onions, diced

4 cloves garlic, chopped

One 3-inch knob of ginger, peeled and grated

8 ounces shiitake mushrooms, stemmed and caps sliced

1 teaspoon kosher salt

¼ teaspoon cayenne pepper

5 cups Basic Chicken Stock (page 55) or Roasted Vegetable Stock (page 56)

1 small head Napa cabbage, thinly sliced

½ jalapeño pepper, seeded and minced

1 tablespoon toasted sesame oil

2 tablespoons brown rice vinegar

Soak the cashews in 3 cups cold water to cover for 8 hours.

Heat the olive oil in a large soup pot over medium-high heat. Add the onions and sauté until translucent, about 5 minutes. Add the garlic, ginger, mushrooms, salt, and cayenne, and cook for about 5 more minutes.

Pour in the stock and add the cabbage and jalapeño. Bring to a boil. Meanwhile, drain the cashews. In a food processor, blend the cashews with 1 cup water until smooth. Strain through a fine-mesh sieve and add to the pot, stirring well. Lower the heat under the pot and simmer the soup, covered, for 20 minutes. (At this point the soup can be refrigerated for up to 3 days or frozen for 1 month.)

Turn off the heat and stir in the sesame oil and rice vinegar. Serve in warmed bowls garnished with a couple of cashew halves.

# hot and sour soup

SERVES 10

Far from your typical hot and sour soup found on Chinese restaurant menus, this recipe is packed with vegetables and flavor. Sugar, MSG, cornstarch, and soy from the standard recipe have been omitted, but all the wonderful flavor remains. My children love this soup, and it is a great way to get them to have vegetables.

¾ cup peanut oil

8 ounces pork shoulder, cut into thin slices

Salt

2 cups fresh shiitake mushrooms, stemmed and caps sliced

4 jalapeño chiles, seeded and minced

3 tablespoons grated fresh ginger

2 tablespoons minced garlic

8 cups Basic Chicken Stock (page 55)

1 small head bok choy, white and green parts, sliced

3 scallions, white and green parts, sliced diagonally, plus extra for garnish

2 large eggs, beaten lightly

1 tablespoon toasted sesame oil

¼ cup brown rice vinegar or apple cider vinegar

½ cup chopped fresh cilantro, plus extra whole sprigs for garnish

Freshly ground pepper

Heat the peanut oil in a soup pot over medium-high heat and add the pork. Season with salt. Sear and brown the meat, about 12 minutes. Use a slotted spoon to transfer the pork to a plate and set aside. Add the shiitake mushrooms, chiles, ginger, and garlic, and cook for 2 minutes. Pour in the stock, add the bok choy and scallions, and return the pork to the pot. Bring to a boil and then slowly stir in the eggs. Turn off the heat and add the sesame oil, vinegar, and cilantro. Add salt and pepper to taste. Stir well and serve in big bowls with a sprig of cilantro or sliced scallions.

# chilled cucumber soup with yogurt and dill

SERVES 6 TO 8

This delightful summer soup is refreshing and delicious as part of a light lunch, perhaps featuring Broiled Orange-Mustard–Glazed Salmon (page 99).

6 large cucumbers, peeled, seeded, and roughly chopped

2 cups Homemade Yogurt (page 27)

¼ cup fresh dill, plus 6 to 8 whole sprigs for garnish

¼ cup fresh mint

¼ cup fresh parsley

¼ cup freshly squeezed lemon juice (about 1 lemon)

2 cloves garlic

2 tablespoons extra-virgin olive oil

1 teaspoon celery salt

1 teaspoon salt to taste

Pinch of cayenne pepper, or more to taste

6 to 8 slices lemon, for garnish

Combine the cucumbers, yogurt, dill, mint, parsley, lemon juice, garlic, olive oil, celery salt, salt and cayenne pepper in a large bowl. Working in batches, place the mixture in the bowl of a food processor or blender and process until pureed. Adjust the seasonings. Chill in the refrigerator for at least 30 minutes or overnight.

Serve in chilled bowls or pretty glasses (martini or dessert). Garnish with a sprig of dill or mint and place a lemon slice over the edge.

# chilled pea soup

The dazzling green color of this healthy, delicious soup helps dress up any table.

**2 tablespoons unsalted butter**
**1 small yellow onion, diced**
**5 cups shelled fresh peas (3 pounds fresh peas) or frozen peas**
**¾ cup Homemade Cream Yogurt (page 27), plus extra for garnish**
**2 tablespoons fresh chopped mint, plus extra whole leaves for garnish**
**Salt and freshly ground pepper**

Melt the butter in a medium saucepan over low heat. Add the onion and cook until translucent, about 7 minutes. Add 2½ cups cold water, bring to a boil, and then lower the heat so the water simmers. Add the peas and simmer for about 10 minutes.

Remove from the heat and add the yogurt and mint. Place in a blender or food processor in batches and puree until smooth. Add salt and pepper to taste. Chill in the refrigerator until cold, at least 3 hours or overnight. Serve cold, garnished with a dollop of yogurt and mint leaves.

# gazpacho

The traditional Sevillian way to prepare and serve gazpacho is with stale bread, a strained soup base, and a variety of condiments to sprinkle on top. It is truly delicious, although quite a lot of work and, of course, off-limits for those on this diet because of the bread. Here is a quick no-bread version that is every bit as delicious as the classic.

2 pounds ripe tomatoes (about 4 or 5), seeded and roughly chopped

3 large cucumbers, peeled, seeded, and roughly chopped

2 green bell peppers, seeded and roughly chopped

1 red or orange bell pepper, seeded and roughly chopped

1 medium red onion, roughly chopped

2 cloves garlic, minced

1 medium bunch flat-leaf parsley, roughly chopped

½ cup extra-virgin olive oil

¼ cup red wine vinegar

2 teaspoons salt

1 teaspoon freshly ground pepper

In a large bowl combine the tomatoes, cucumbers, bell peppers, onion, garlic, parsley, olive oil, vinegar, salt, and pepper.

Place in a food processor or blender in batches and process until fairly smooth but still a little chunky in texture. Taste and adjust the seasonings. Chill for at least 1 hour or overnight. Serve in chilled martini glasses or bowls.

# sauces, spreads, dips, and dressings

Lucques Olive Tapenade

Cucumber Raita

Lemon-Parsley-Ginger Dressing

Classic French Vinaigrette

Asian Dressing

**you may have to be more conscious** of what you eat, but there is absolutely no reason to eat bland food. The sauces, spreads, dips, and dressings in this chapter have the ability to transform a dish without the sugars, starches, and other additives found in many bottled condiments.

The sauces can be used on a variety of grilled and roasted meats, fish, and vegetables, as well as on many of the Mock Starches, including Pizza Margherita (page 169) and Pasta Aglio Oglio with Enoki Mushrooms (page 167). Try the diet-approved Aïoli (page 82) or Homemade Dijon Mustard (page 80) as a spread for sandwiches or alongside steamed artichokes, and you'll never want to go back to store-bought again.

Finally, the flavorful dressings and vinaigrettes in this chapter, including Lemon-Parsley-Ginger Dressing (page 89), Classic French Vinaigrette (page 90), and Asian Dressing (page 91), really pack a punch. Experiment by trying different varieties on the salads in this book and on some of your own favorite salads, grilled and steamed vegetables, and grilled fish and chicken.

# classic tomato sauce

MAKES 6 CUPS

This is an easy tomato sauce that will soon become a staple in your kitchen.
Use it for pizzas, mock pastas, casseroles, and more. This sauce contains
no sugars or starches and tastes much better than any store-bought variety.
The recipe easily doubles and freezes well for up to four months.

¼ cup olive oil
1 small onion, chopped
6 cloves garlic, chopped
1 carrot, peeled and chopped
Salt and freshly ground pepper to taste
Two 28-ounce cans or cartons Italian whole tomatoes
1 bay leaf
2 tablespoons unsalted butter
1 cup fresh basil

Heat the oil in a large saucepan over medium-high heat. Add the onion and cook until
translucent, about 5 minutes. Add the garlic and cook for another minute. Add the carrot,
salt, and pepper, and cook for 10 more minutes, stirring occasionally to prevent burning.
Add the tomatoes and bay leaf, lower the heat, and simmer for 1 hour, uncovered.

Remove the bay leaf and stir in the butter.

When the sauce has cooled somewhat, place in a food processor or blender in batches
and puree with the basil. Adjust the seasoning with salt and pepper.

Reheat if needed and serve immediately or store in an airtight container in the refrigerator for up to 1 week or in the freezer for up to 4 months. Reheat before serving.

# spinach, lemon, and basil pesto

MAKES 1 CUP

This vibrant green pesto is delicious as a garnish for soups, as a spread for sandwiches, and as a dip for vegetables. The lemon gives it a lovely tanginess. Try it on grilled tuna or chicken, and on any vegetable "spaghetti."

1½ cups fresh basil
½ cup fresh spinach
1 tablespoon grated lemon zest
½ cup freshly grated Parmesan cheese
½ cup extra-virgin olive oil
½ cup freshly squeezed lemon juice (2 to 3 lemons)
¼ cup walnuts, toasted
4 cloves garlic
Salt and freshly ground pepper to taste

In a food processor or blender, combine the basil, spinach, lemon zest, Parmesan cheese, olive oil, lemon juice, walnuts, garlic, salt and pepper and puree until smooth. The pesto can be kept in a sealed container in the refrigerator for up to 1 week or in the freezer for up to 4 months.

# fresh mint sauce

MAKES 1½ CUPS

This homemade sauce is so much tastier than cloyingly sweet, neon-colored, store-bought mint jellies made with sugars and artificial coloring. Serve this delicious condiment with lamb, grilled meats, and grilled vegetables.

1 cup fresh mint
3 tablespoons apple cider vinegar
3 tablespoons freshly squeezed orange juice
2 tablespoons honey
Salt and pepper to taste
¼ cup extra-virgin olive oil

In a food processor or a blender, puree the mint, vinegar, juice, honey, salt, and pepper. While blending, slowly pour in the oil and process until smooth.

# hollandaise sauce

MAKES 1 CUP

Delicious on Eggs Florentine Benedict (page 199) or served alongside grilled asparagus or as a dip for steamed artichokes, this rich sauce is very versatile. Although the eggs are heated to make the sauce, as an extra precaution to protect against salmonella, I boil the eggs quickly before using them in the recipe.

**8 large eggs**
**2 tablespoons freshly squeezed lemon juice**
**¾ cup clarified butter (see box)**
**Salt and freshly ground pepper**

In a medium saucepan, cover the eggs with cold water and bring to a boil. Cook for 1 minute. Scoop out the eggs using a slotted spoon and transfer to a bowl of cold water to cool. Reserve the saucepan of boiling water over low heat.

Crack the eggs and use a teaspoon to scoop the yolks into a medium stainless steel bowl. Add the juice and immediately whisk vigorously to combine. Place the bowl over the saucepan of simmering water (the water should not touch the bowl; pour some out if you have too much) and continue whisking. You do not want the eggs to get too hot and scramble. Slowly pour the butter in, a little at a time, still whisking, until all the butter has been added and the sauce has increased in volume and thickened.

Remove from the heat and add salt and pepper to taste. Strain through a fine-mesh strainer and use immediately. If made in advance, the sauce can be stored in a thermos for up to 3 hours.

## CLARIFIED BUTTER

Melt the butter in a small saucepan over low heat without browning. Turn off the heat. Allow the butter to sit for a minute, then skim the milk solids off the top and discard. Two sticks (1 cup) unsalted butter will yield approximately ¾ cup clarified butter.

# carrot-ginger paste

MAKES 1 CUP

This vibrant orange condiment is excellent on mock pasta, pulsed zucchini or cashews, steamed vegetables, chicken, and fish. Stir some into a simple vinaigrette for a color and flavor boost. It also makes a wonderful topping for Asian-style soups and homemade broths.

**3 large carrots, peeled and chopped**
**One 2-inch knob of fresh ginger, peeled**
**3 cloves garlic**
**1 tablespoon roasted tahini**
**¼ cup freshly squeezed lemon juice (about 1 lemon)**
**Salt to taste**
**Cayenne pepper to taste**

Puree the carrots, ginger, garlic, tahini, lemon juice, salt, and cayenne pepper in a food processor. You can leave the mixture a bit chunky or make it completely smooth as you prefer. Refrigerate in a sealed glass jam jar for up to 3 days.

## variations:

Substitute peeled raw beets for the carrots and use ½ cup cilantro, parsley, or chives in place of the ginger.

Substitute orange, lime, or grapefruit juice for the lemon juice.

# roasted red pepper spread

MAKES 1 CUP

This spread really jazzes up a sandwich or a cracker and is perfect with cheeses and as a dip for vegetables.

2 large red bell peppers, roasted (see box)

5 cloves garlic

1 teaspoon ground cumin

2 tablespoons fresh parsley

2 tablespoons freshly squeezed lemon juice

Salt and freshly ground pepper to taste

¼ cup extra-virgin olive oil

In a food processor or blender, puree the peppers, garlic, cumin, parsley, juice, salt, and pepper until smooth. While the machine is running, slowly pour in the oil and process until incorporated.

## ROASTED PEPPERS

Preheat the broiler.

Place the peppers under the broiler and turn periodically as needed, until charred on all sides. Put the peppers in a closed brown paper bag for a few minutes to help loosen their skins, then peel, core, and seed the peppers. Serve immediately or store in a jar with a tight-fitting lid in the refrigerator for up to 1 week.

# homemade dijon mustard

MAKES 1 CUP

Rather than relying on store-bought mustards, which often contain sugar and artificial coloring, make your own. It's easy! The following recipe is also the base for a bunch of variations (see below). Try adding any of the following to your homemade mustard for endless variations: chopped chives, orange juice, chopped capers, crushed peppercorns, chopped shallots, sugar-free cranberry sauce, cayenne pepper, chopped fresh basil, Indian spices, and more. Place in pretty jars and give them as gifts.

**2 cups dry white wine**
**1 medium white or yellow onion, chopped**
**3 cloves garlic, chopped**
**1 cup pure ground mustard**
**3 tablespoons honey**
**1 tablespoon olive oil**
**2 teaspoons salt**

Combine the wine, onion, and garlic in a medium saucepan. Bring to a boil over medium heat, then lower the heat and simmer for 5 minutes. Remove from the heat and set aside to cool. Strain, discarding the solids.

Put the ground mustard in a bowl and add the wine mixture, stirring vigorously until smooth. Stir in the honey, oil, and salt.

Return the mixture to the saucepan and heat over low heat, stirring, until it is thickened, about 3 to 5 minutes. Make sure you hold your face away from the pungent steam, because it can burn your nasal passages.

Cool completely and store in a jar with a tight-fitting lid in the refrigerator for up to 3 months.

**lemon garlic mustard**

Stir in 1 tablespoon minced garlic, 1 teaspoon grated lemon zest, 2 tablespoons freshly squeezed lemon juice, 2 teaspoons honey, and 1 teaspoon olive oil.

**honey mustard**

Stir in 1 cup honey and ¾ cup ground mustard. Makes 2½ cups.

**tarragon mustard**

Add ¾ cup fresh tarragon leaves and 1 tablespoon dry white wine. Puree in a food processor until smooth.

**horseradish mustard**

In a food processor, add 5 tablespoons extra-virgin olive oil, ¼ cup white wine vinegar, 2 tablespoons peeled and grated fresh horseradish, pinch of grated lemon zest, 2 tablespoons freshly squeezed lemon juice, and a pinch of salt. Process until smooth.

# aïoli

MAKES 1 CUP

This delicious, versatile sauce can be used as a base for salad dressings and dips, a spread for sandwiches, and essentially anything that you would use mayonnaise for. Unlike the classic recipe that uses raw eggs, the eggs in this recipe are cooked to avoid the chance of getting salmonella poisoning. This makes the sauce a good deal less thick but no less tasty.

**2 extra-large eggs**
**1 teaspoon Homemade Dijon Mustard (page 80)**
**¼ cup freshly squeezed lemon juice (about 1 lemon)**
**1 clove garlic, minced**
**Salt and freshly ground pepper to taste**
**1 cup extra-virgin olive oil**

Place the eggs in a small saucepan filled with cold water. Bring to a boil and boil for 1 minute. Drain the eggs and immediately plunge into a bowl of cold water.

Crack the eggs and use a teaspoon to scoop the yolks into a food processor or electric mixer; discard the whites. Add the mustard, juice, garlic, salt, and pepper, and blend. While the machine is running, slowly add the oil. Adjust the seasoning if needed with additional salt and pepper. Refrigerate in a sealed container for up to 3 days.

# yogurt curry dip

This is a lovely, creamy, spicy dip for vegetables or Buttery Herb and Garlic Crackers (page 159). It is also a good topping for soups and salads.

**2 cups Strained Yogurt (page 28)**
**¼ cup freshly squeezed lemon juice (about 1 lemon)**
**1 large shallot, finely chopped**
**2 tablespoons snipped chives**
**2 teaspoons curry powder**
**1 teaspoon ground turmeric**
**1 teaspoon celery salt, or more to taste**

In a medium bowl, stir together the yogurt, lemon juice, shallot, chives, curry powder, turmeric, and salt. The dip can be stored in a sealed container in the refrigerator for up to 1 week.

# white bean hummus

MAKES 2 CUPS

I absolutely love the smooth protein-packed taste of hummus, so I made it my mission to find a substitute for the "illegal" starchy garbanzo beans. Navy beans proved to be a delicious alternative.

1½ cups dried white navy beans
6 cloves Roasted Garlic (see box)
2 tablespoons tahini
1 tablespoon ground cumin
½ cup freshly squeezed lemon juice (2 to 3 lemons)
Celery salt and freshly ground pepper to taste
½ to ¾ cup extra-virgin olive oil
Pinch of paprika or cayenne pepper for garnish (optional)

Rinse and pick over the beans to remove any small pebbles, and then soak in water for 24 hours, changing the water halfway through. Rinse and drain.

Put the beans in a large pot with 5 or 6 cups fresh water to cover. Bring to a boil over high heat. Lower the heat so that the water boils gently and cook for 1 hour, or until soft. Skim off any foam or bean skins that rise to the surface.

Drain the beans. Prepare the roasted garlic. Transfer the beans and garlic to a food processor and puree with the tahini, cumin, juice, celery salt, and pepper. With the machine running, slowly drizzle in ½ cup oil through the feed tube. Puree until smooth. This makes a thick hummus. If you prefer a thinner one, add ¼ cup oil.

Transfer to a bowl and sprinkle with paprika before serving if desired. The hummus can be stored in the refrigerator in a sealed container for up to 1 week.

## ROASTED GARLIC

1 large head garlic
1 teaspoon olive oil
Pinch of kosher salt
Pinch of pepper

Preheat the oven to 350°F.

Cut the top off a head of garlic so that the bulbs are exposed. Rub the exposed bulbs with the oil and season with salt and pepper.

Place the garlic in a ramekin or a small ovenproof dish. Roast for 1 hour or until golden and very soft. Allow to cool. When cool enough to handle, squeeze out the garlic paste. Refrigerate the garlic in a sealed container for up to 1 week.

# artichoke dip

This easy, flavorful dip is delicious with Roasted Vegetables (page 40) and with Lime and Sea Salt Tortilla Chips (page 156). Try it in place of mayonnaise on sandwiches.

**Two 8½-ounce cans artichoke hearts, packed in water, rinsed and drained**
**4 cloves garlic**
**¼ cup freshly grated Parmesan cheese**
**¼ cup freshly squeezed lemon juice (about 1 lemon)**
**Salt and pepper to taste**
**¼ cup olive oil**

Place the artichoke hearts, garlic, Parmesan, juice, salt, and pepper in a food processor and process until finely chopped. With the machine running, slowly drizzle in the oil through the feed tube. Transfer to a serving bowl or store in a lidded jar in the refrigerator for up to 1 week.

# lucques olive tapenade

MAKES 1 CUP

My mother used to make delicious tangy and salty chopped olive sandwiches for me for lunch. The other kids at school thought it was odd, but I knew better. Today I still love them, especially on Cashew Bread (page 160). You can use this rich olive spread as a dip and as a topping for soup, too.

**1 cup Lucques, or your favorite brine-cured olives (Kalamatas also work great), pitted**
**2 cloves garlic, peeled**
**1 tablespoon capers, drained**
**1 tablespoon grated lemon zest**
**2 tablespoons freshly squeezed lemon juice**
**2 tablespoons extra-virgin olive oil**
**Salt and freshly ground pepper to taste**

In a food processor, process the olives, garlic, capers, lemon zest and juice, olive oil, salt and pepper until finely chopped but not completely smooth. The tapenade can be stored in the refrigerator in a sealed container for up to 1 week.

# cucumber raita

MAKES 3 CUPS

This is a wonderful Indian-inspired side dish to serve with any spicy food. It cools the palate and helps the digestive system deal with the spicy food. It is also great as a dip and on its own.

1½ cups Strained Yogurt (page 28)
2 medium cucumbers, peeled, seeded, and chopped
3 tablespoons finely chopped red onion
3 tablespoons finely chopped fresh cilantro
3 tablespoons finely chopped fresh mint
3 tablespoons freshly squeezed lemon juice
1 teaspoon ground cumin
Celery salt and freshly ground pepper to taste

In a medium bowl, stir together the yogurt, cucumbers, onion, cilantro, mint, lemon juice, cumin, celery salt, and pepper. The raita can be refrigerated in a sealed container for up to 2 days.

# lemon-parsley-ginger dressing

MAKES ¾ CUP

This tangy dressing gives a kick to any salad or grilled or steamed vegetables.

**4 cloves garlic**
**One 2-inch knob peeled fresh ginger**
**½ cup fresh parsley**
**¼ cup freshly squeezed lemon juice (about 1 lemon)**
**Salt and freshly ground pepper to taste**
**½ cup extra-virgin olive oil**

Puree the garlic, ginger, parsley, juice, salt, and pepper in a blender or food processor. While the motor is running, slowly add the oil and process until incorporated. The dressing can be refrigerated in a sealed container for up to 1 week.

# classic french vinaigrette

MAKES ¾ CUP

This traditional recipe, composed of red wine vinegar, mustard, chopped shallot, and olive oil, is the perfect accompaniment to a simple mixed lettuce salad or a composed and elaborate salad such as Salad Niçoise with Grilled Ahi (page 50).

¼ **cup red wine vinegar**
**1 tablespoon Homemade Dijon Mustard (page 80)**
**2 tablespoons minced shallots**
**Salt and freshly ground pepper to taste**
½ **cup extra-virgin olive oil**

In a bowl, whisk together the vinegar, mustard, shallots, salt, and pepper. Slowly whisk in the oil until incorporated. Adjust the seasonings.

The vinaigrette will keep in a glass jar with a tight-fitting lid in the refrigerator for up to 5 days.

# asian dressing

MAKES 1 CUP

This delicious dressing is wonderful on a variety of salads, vegetables, and grilled chicken or fish.

1 tablespoon minced garlic

1 tablespoon grated fresh ginger

1 green or red chile, seeds removed and minced

1 tablespoon black sesame seeds (if tolerated), toasted (see page 53)

1 tablespoon roasted tahini

1 tablespoon date paste or 2 Medjool dates mashed with a fork

1 teaspoon cayenne pepper

¼ cup freshly squeezed lemon juice (about 1 lemon)

⅛ cup freshly squeezed lime juice (about 1 lime)

⅛ cup freshly squeezed orange juice

2 tablespoons toasted sesame oil

Salt and freshly ground pepper to taste

Whisk together the garlic, ginger, chile, sesame seeds, tahini, date paste, cayenne, lemon juice, lime juice, orange juice, and the sesame oil in a small mixing bowl. Season with salt and pepper. Serve immediately or store in a glass jar with a tight-fitting lid in the refrigerator for up to 3 days.

# fish and shellfish

Whole Roasted Red Snapper Stuffed with Fennel and Citrus

Tilapia Curry with Saffron

Sauteéd Fillet of Sole with Lemon, Butter, and Capers

Broiled Orange-Mustard–Glazed Salmon

Banana Leaf–Wrapped Halibut with Papaya and Coconut

Swordfish Steaks with Mango Salsa

Seared Ahi Tuna Tartare with Sesame, Avocado, and Ginger

Steamed Clams in White Wine, Thyme, and Butter

Shellfish Paella with Zucchini Rice and Homemade Chorizo

**fish and shellfish are wonderful sources** of protein that are low in fat and high in essential nutrients, minerals, and fatty acids, all of which our bodies need.

A few rules apply when it comes to buying fish. First, always be sure to buy the freshest, best-quality fish available. Smell the fish before you purchase it. If it smells "fishy" or the gills are gray, pass on it. The fish called for in the recipes in this chapter can easily be substituted with similar fish, so be sure to use what is freshest that day at the market. Look for wild fish and shellfish rather than the farm-raised variety whenever possible. Farm-raised fish and shellfish often contain harmful toxins, and not only is wild fish better for you, but it also tastes better. Be sure to purchase fish the same day you plan to cook it. Bacteria can grow on fish that has been sitting around a few days, even if refrigerated.

You should also be aware of the high mercury levels in many types of fish. The bigger the fish (swordfish, shark, and tuna are some examples), the more mercury it contains, so try not to consume these varieties too often. Removing the skin from the fish and grilling or broiling helps reduce mercury levels (the mercury drips away).

The fish and shellfish in these recipes are easily found in your local market or fish store.

# whole roasted red snapper stuffed with fennel and citrus

SERVES 4

This Mediterranean dish combines the distinct flavors of fennel and orange with sea bass and a variety of delicate herbs. It is wonderful on its own or served with Pasta Aglio Oglio with Enoki Mushrooms (page 167).

3 tablespoons olive oil

1 medium fennel bulb, trimmed and sliced, and fronds reserved

Salt and freshly ground pepper

2 cloves garlic, chopped

½ cup dry white wine

1 tablespoon grated orange zest

½ cup freshly squeezed orange juice (1 to 2 oranges)

One 4-pound red snapper, scaled and gutted

2 lemons

1 small bunch fresh thyme

1 small bunch fresh marjoram (optional)

½ cup chopped fresh parsley

Preheat the oven to 400°F.

Heat 1 tablespoon oil in a large skillet over high heat. Add the fennel, sprinkle with salt and pepper, and add the garlic. Pour in the wine and add the orange zest and juice. Cover and lower the heat. Simmer for about 20 minutes, until just done and opaque. Remove from the heat and cool in the liquid.

Lay the snapper on a parchment-covered roasting pan. Season the inside of the fish with salt and pepper. Slice one of the lemons and lay the lemon slices, thyme, marjoram, and the cooled fennel and its liquid inside the fish. Tie the fish at 2-inch intervals with butcher's twine. Rub the remaining 2 tablespoons oil all over the fish and sprinkle with salt and pepper. Slash the skin in 5 places on each side.

Measure the thickest part of the fish and roast for 15 minutes per inch, approximately 15 to 20 minutes. Check for doneness by lifting the flesh at the thickest part with a knife to make sure it is opaque.

Transfer to a serving platter and garnish with fennel fronds and parsley. Cut the remaining lemon into wedges and serve alongside.

# tilapia curry with saffron

This dish takes fish and vegetable curry to a new dimension with the infusion of saffron and aromatic Indian spices. Serve with French Lentil Salad (page 54) if desired.

2 medium yellow onions, roughly chopped

3 tablespoons roughly chopped fresh ginger

10 cloves garlic, roughly chopped

10 whole cloves

2 cinnamon sticks

2 bay leaves

¼ cup olive oil

1½ tablespoons ground cumin

1½ tablespoons ground coriander

1 tablespoon ground cardamom

1 teaspoon turmeric

½ teaspoon cayenne pepper

1½ teaspoons salt

2 medium zucchini, chopped

1 small head cauliflower, broken into bite-sized florets

1 small butternut squash, peeled, seeded, and chopped

One 28-ounce can or carton Italian chopped tomatoes

1 cup Homemade Yogurt (page 27)

2 pounds tilapia, red snapper, or halibut fillet, cut into 2-inch pieces

1½ teaspoons saffron, crumbled

6 lime wedges

½ cup chopped fresh cilantro

Place the onions, ginger, garlic, and 2 tablespoons water in a blender or food processor and blend until you have a smooth paste.

Tie the cloves, cinnamon sticks, and bay leaves in cheesecloth.

Heat the oil in a large stockpot over medium-high heat. Add the cumin, coriander, cardamom, turmeric, and cayenne. Cook for 1 minute, stirring. Add the salt and onion paste, and fry about 8 minutes more, until light golden brown.

Add the zucchini, cauliflower, squash, tomatoes, yogurt, and 1 cup water. Stir well. Cover and simmer for 20 minutes, stirring occasionally, until the vegetables are tender.

Meanwhile, soak the saffron in ½ cup warm water for 20 minutes.

After 20 minutes, place the fish and saffron water in the stockpot and stir gently to submerge the fish and distribute the saffron. Cover and simmer over low heat for 10 minutes.

Serve immediately in soup bowls and garnish with the lime wedges and cilantro.

# sautéed fillet of sole with lemon, butter, and capers

SERVES 4

This flaky white fish is served here in the classic French tradition but with ground almonds replacing the bread crumb. This mild preparation will help encourage kids to eat fish.

**Four 8-ounce fillets of sole**
**Salt and freshly ground pepper**
**1½ cups almond flour**
**2 large eggs, beaten**
**6 tablespoons unsalted butter**
**3 tablespoons olive oil**
**3 tablespoons drained capers**
**2 tablespoons grated lemon zest**
**½ cup freshly squeezed lemon juice (2 to 3 lemons)**
**¼ cup finely chopped fresh parsley**
**4 lemon wedges**

Season the fish with salt and pepper. Dip in almond flour and then in egg, shaking off any excess.

Heat 2 tablespoons butter and 1 tablespoon oil in a large skillet. Cook the fish over medium-high heat for 3 or 4 minutes on each side, until golden brown and cooked through. Arrange on heated plates.

Discard the oil and butter in the pan and wipe the pan with paper towels. Heat on high and add the remaining 4 tablespoons butter and 2 tablespoons oil. Add the capers and zest, and cook for 30 seconds. Add the juice, stir, and then drizzle over the fish. Sprinkle with parsley, garnish with lemon wedges, and serve.

# broiled orange-mustard–glazed salmon

SERVES 6

I encourage you to buy wild salmon, not farm-raised. Not only is it better for you, but it also tastes so much better. Salmon has a rich, fatty flavor and texture, and the sweet-tart-spicy orange-mustard topping complements it perfectly.

**1 tablespoon grated orange zest**
**½ cup freshly squeezed orange juice (about 1 orange)**
**4 tablespoons olive oil**
**3 tablespoons honey**
**2 tablespoons Homemade Dijon Mustard (page 80)**
**3 cloves garlic, minced**
**Salt and freshly ground pepper to taste**
**Six 6- to 8-ounce wild salmon fillets, skin removed**

Place the zest, juice, 2 tablespoons oil, honey, mustard, garlic, salt, and pepper in a blender or food processor and process until smooth. Set aside. (Can be made 1 day in advance.)

Preheat the broiler.

Rub the fillets with the remaining 2 tablespoons of oil and season with salt and pepper. Broil for 2 to 4 minutes on each side, depending on the thickness of the fillet, until lightly browned but still underdone in the center. Brush the salmon with the orange glaze and broil for another 2 minutes, until golden and cooked to medium. Serve immediately.

# banana leaf–wrapped halibut with papaya and coconut

SERVES 6

These aromatic packages make a beautiful presentation. Let guests unwrap them at the table for the full effect. Banana leaves can be found in Asian markets, but you can substitute parchment paper if necessary.

**6 large banana leaves or sheets of parchment paper**

**2 tablespoons olive oil**

**1 small red onion, minced**

**2 cloves garlic, minced**

**One 2-inch knob fresh ginger, peeled and cut into thin matchsticks**

**3 scallions, thinly sliced on the diagonal**

**1 red bell pepper, thinly sliced**

**1 ripe papaya, peeled, seeded, and cut into matchsticks**

**Meat of ½ fresh coconut, thinly sliced**

**3 tablespoons toasted sesame oil**

**Salt to taste**

**Cayenne pepper to taste**

**Six 6- to 8-ounce halibut fillets**

**2 limes (preferably Kaffir), sliced**

**2 stalks lemongrass, each cut into 3 pieces and smashed**

**1 cup fresh or canned unsweetened coconut milk**

**6 toothpicks**

Preheat the oven to 450° F.

Open up the banana leaves and rub them with the olive oil. Divide in half the onion, garlic, ginger, scallions, bell pepper, papaya, coconut, sesame oil, salt, and cayenne. Scatter one half along the center of the leaves, lay the halibut fillets on top, and then scatter the remaining half on top. Place 2 or 3 lime slices on each serving and 1 stalk smashed lemongrass. Pour coconut milk on top of each portion. Wrap the leaves like a package, folding the top and bottom over each other and then the sides. Secure with a toothpick.

Pour about ½ inch of water in a 9 × 13-inch pan fitted with a rack. Place the halibut bundles on the rack, cover with foil, and steam in the oven for 20 minutes. Remove the bundles from the oven and place on 6 soup plates. Open each bundle and remove the lime slices and lemongrass stalk before eating.

# swordfish steaks with mango salsa

SERVES 4

This simple grilled firm fish is elevated by the bright flavor of the mango salsa. You might also try serving the salsa alongside grilled chicken or grilled vegetables.

**4 tablespoons olive oil**

**Four 8-ounce swordfish steaks, each about 1 inch thick**

**Salt and freshly ground pepper**

**1 large ripe mango, diced**

**1 small red onion, diced**

**1 Hass avocado, diced**

**½ cup chopped fresh cilantro**

**2 cloves garlic, minced**

**1 jalapeño pepper, seeds removed and minced**

**¼ cup freshly squeezed lime or lemon juice**

Heat the grill to high.

Using 2 tablespoons oil, coat the swordfish steaks all over. Season with salt and pepper. Grill for about 8 minutes per side, until browned and cooked through.

While the fish is cooking, mix together the remaining 2 tablespoons oil, mango, onion, avocado, cilantro, garlic, jalapeño, and lime juice. Set aside.

When the swordfish steaks are cooked, arrange them on heated plates and top with a generous mound of mango salsa.

# seared ahi tuna tartare with sesame, avocado, and ginger

The velvety yet substantial texture of tuna combines here with the strong and subtle flavors of ginger, citrus, and honey.

8 ounces fresh sushi-grade Ahi tuna steaks

Salt

Pinch of cayenne pepper

2 tablespoons toasted sesame oil

1 clove garlic, minced

1 tablespoon freshly grated ginger

1 tablespoon grated orange zest

¼ cup freshly squeezed orange juice

¼ cup freshly squeezed lemon juice (about 1 lemon)

1 tablespoon Homemade Dijon Mustard (page 80) or wasabi

1 tablespoon honey

2 Hass avocados, peeled, pitted, and cubed

½ small red onion, minced

1 tablespoon snipped fresh chives

2 tablespoons currants

½ cup fresh chopped cilantro

1 tablespoon black sesame seeds (if tolerated), toasted (see page 53)

Freshly ground pepper to taste

Heat the grill to high.

Season the tuna steaks with salt and cayenne. Grill for 2 or 3 minutes per side for rare. Set on a cutting board and let rest for 5 minutes.

In a small bowl, combine the sesame oil, garlic, ginger, zest, juices, and mustard. Set aside.

Cut the fish into small dice and set in a medium bowl. Add the honey, avocados, onion, chives, currants, half of the cilantro, and half of the sesame seeds. Season with salt and pepper. Pour the dressing on top and mix thoroughly.

Place the mixture on a serving platter or bowl or divide among individual plates. Top with the remaining sesame seeds and cilantro.

# steamed clams in white wine, thyme, and butter

SERVES 4

When I was a kid, my cousins, brothers, sister, and I would go clamming on the beach in Santa Barbara and come home with bucketfuls of fresh clams. My mother would whip up this delicious dish for everyone on Sunday afternoons. It was a great end to our weekends at the beach. The only change I've made to my mother's dish is that now I serve this with toasted Cashew Bread (page 160) to sop up the juices.

1 cup salt
4 dozen (about 8 pounds) Littleneck clams, scrubbed
3 tablespoons olive oil
2 large shallots, chopped
4 cloves garlic, chopped
3 tablespoons chopped fresh thyme
2 cups dry white wine
3 tablespoons unsalted butter
¼ cup finely chopped fresh parsley

Dissolve the salt in 3 quarts of water. Add the clams and soak overnight in the refrigerator to remove grit, then drain and rinse them.

Heat the oil in a large pot over medium heat and add the shallots. Cook for 1 minute and then add the garlic and thyme. Cook for 1 more minute, then pour in the wine and add the clams. Cover and simmer for about 10 minutes, or until all the clams have opened; discard any that do not open.

Stir in the butter and parsley. Serve 1 dozen clams with broth per person.

# shellfish paella with zucchini rice and homemade chorizo

SERVES 6 TO 8

Finely chopped zucchini substitutes for the rice in this otherwise relatively classic Spanish dish. The array of shellfish, meat, herbs, and vegetables makes this colorful dish a wonderful presentation. The recipe easily doubles or triples to feed a hungry crowd. Serve with a simple green salad and a good Spanish wine.

8 medium zucchini (about 3 pounds), peeled
One 3-pound chicken, cut into 8 pieces, or about 2 pounds chicken parts
Salt and freshly ground pepper to taste
1 tablespoon paprika
¼ cup olive oil
1 pound Homemade Crumbled Chorizo (recipe follows)
2 teaspoons saffron
1 small onion, diced
6 cloves garlic, chopped
1 red bell pepper, chopped
1 large tomato, peeled, seeded, and chopped
1 cup fresh or frozen peas
2 cups Basic Chicken Stock (page 55)
1 pound fresh mussels, scrubbed
1 pound fresh clams, scrubbed
12 large shrimp, shells and veins removed
1 cup chopped fresh flat-leaf parsley
6 to 8 lemon wedges

In a food processor, pulse the zucchini until the pieces are the size of grains of rice. Wrap the zucchini in a tea towel and squeeze out the water. Set aside.

Preheat the oven to 300° F.

Season the chicken with salt, pepper, and paprika.

Heat the oil in a paella pan or very large skillet over medium heat. Add the chicken pieces and cook until browned all over, about 10 minutes. With a slotted spoon, remove the chicken to a roasting pan and transfer to the oven for 20 minutes, until cooked through.

Drain off all but 1 tablespoon of fat from the pan. Add the chorizo to the pan and cook for 5 minutes, until brown. Using a slotted spoon, remove the chorizo to a bowl and set aside.

Soak the saffron in ¼ cup warm water.

Add the onion to the pan and cook over medium heat for 2 minutes. Add the garlic and cook for 1 more minute. Add the red pepper, tomato, and peas, and cook for 2 minutes. Add the zucchini to the pan and cook for 2 minutes. Add the stock, stir, and simmer for 15 minutes.

Return the chicken and chorizo to the pan. Add the saffron and its soaking liquid. Stir in the mussels, clams, and shrimp. Simmer for 10 minutes, until the mussels and clams open; discard any that do not open.

Season with salt and pepper. Sprinkle fresh parsley on top and serve hot with lemon wedges on the side.


## HOMEMADE CRUMBLED CHORIZO

**MAKES ABOUT 1 POUND OR 2½ CUPS**

This makes a flavorful addition to many dishes. Try adding it to scrambled eggs, homemade quesadillas, or soups.

**1 tablespoon ground cumin**
**1 tablespoon dried oregano**
**1 tablespoon chile powder**
**1 tablespoon dried thyme**
**1 tablespoon paprika**
**3 tablespoons minced onion**
**2 tablespoons minced fresh garlic**
**1 pound ground pork**
**1 teaspoon salt**
**½ teaspoon freshly ground pepper**

Toast the cumin, oregano, chile powder, thyme, and paprika in a skillet over medium heat until fragrant, 3 to 4 minutes. Transfer to a medium bowl and let cool.

Add the onion, garlic, and pork to the spices and mix well. Add salt and pepper, and mix again. Cover and chill in the refrigerator for at least 3 hours or up to 2 days before cooking.

# poultry and meat

Moroccan Chicken Stew with Cashews, Saffron, and Currants

Green Chicken Curry with Kaffir Limes and Lemongrass

Roast Chicken with Fresh Herbs, Blood Orange, and Paprika

Asian Skewered Peanut Chicken Thighs with Asparagus

Roast Turkey Breast with Fresh Herb Sauce

Papaya-Marinated Grilled Flank Steak

Steak and Vegetable Stir-fry in Lettuce Cups

Ground Beef Chili with Navy Beans

Kibbeh with Yogurt and Mint

Baby Back Ribs with Date-Barbecue Sauce

Roast Pork Loin with Stewed Fruits

Garlic and Rosemary Leg of Lamb

Shepherd's Pie with Mashed Cauliflower

Lamb Keftas with Yogurt Dip

**while following the scd,** you are required to limit your intake of complex sugars and starches, but that doesn't mean you have to limit flavor in the meals you prepare. The entrées in this chapter feature a range of wonderful and exotic flavors, both bold and subtle. They are inspired by different countries of origin, including China (Steak and Vegetable Stir-fry in Lettuce Cups, page 119), Morocco (Moroccan Chicken Stew with Cashews, Saffron, and Currants, page 110), Thailand (Asian Skewered Peanut Chicken Thighs with Asparagus, page 115), France (Garlic and Rosemary Leg of Lamb, page 127), Lebanon (Kibbeh with Yogurt and Mint, page 122), Ireland (Shepherd's Pie with Mashed Cauliflower, page 128), and the United States (Ground Beef Chili with Navy Beans, page 120).

# moroccan chicken stew with cashews, saffron, and currants

SERVES 6 TO 8

This gorgeous savory stew is packed with enticing and foreign flavors. There are surprises in every bite: nuts, olives, and sweet currants. It is the perfect dish for a dinner party because it can be made ahead and reheated.

1 teaspoon saffron

3 pounds boneless, skinless chicken thighs

Salt and freshly ground pepper

½ cup olive oil

1 onion, chopped

10 cloves garlic, chopped

2 tablespoons minced fresh ginger

1 fennel bulb, sliced

2 tablespoons ground cumin

1 tablespoon paprika

¼ teaspoon cayenne pepper

6 cinnamon sticks

One 28-ounce can Italian chopped tomatoes

1 whole cauliflower, cut into florets (about 2 cups)

1 cup currants

1 cup pitted green olives

3 cups Basic Chicken Stock (page 55)

1 tablespoon grated lemon zest

1 cup cashews

¼ cup chopped fresh parsley

1 lemon, cut into 6 to 8 wedges

Bring ¼ cup water to a boil in a small saucepan. Add the saffron, remove from the heat, and set aside for 30 minutes.

Meanwhile, rinse the chicken and pat dry. Season with salt and pepper. Heat 3 tablespoons oil in a large Dutch oven or pot over medium-high heat. Add the chicken and brown on both sides, about 7 minutes per side. Remove the chicken and set aside.

Add 3 more tablespoons oil to the pot and heat over medium heat. Add the onion and cook for 2 minutes. Add the garlic and ginger, and cook for 1 minute. Add the remaining 2 tablespoons oil along with the fennel, cumin, paprika, cayenne, and cinnamon sticks, and stir well. Return the chicken to the pot along with the tomatoes, cauliflower, currants, olives, stock, zest, cashews, and saffron. Cover and cook over low heat for 30 minutes. (The stew can be made ahead up to this point and then cooled and refrigerated for up to 3 days.)

Add the parsley and adjust the seasonings if necessary. Serve in warmed bowls with a lemon wedge on the side.

# green chicken curry with kaffir limes and lemongrass

This Thai-inspired dish bursts with a variety of tangy flavors, including lemon-grass, Kaffir limes, and fresh herbs. Serve with a simple green salad.

### CURRY PASTE

8 to 10 green Thai or Birds Eye chiles, seeded

6 cloves garlic

4 medium shallots

One 2-inch knob fresh ginger, peeled

1 tablespoon grated lime zest

1 teaspoon ground coriander

1 tablespoon peanut oil

1 teaspoon salt

### CHICKEN

3 pounds chicken parts

Salt and freshly ground pepper to taste

3 tablespoons peanut oil

4 ounces button mushrooms, sliced

Three 14.5-ounce cans unsweetened coconut milk

5 Kaffir lime leaves

1 stalk lemongrass, bottom end pounded

6 scallions, white and green parts, sliced on the diagonal

½ cup basil (Asian basil, if possible), cut into thin ribbons

¼ cup chopped fresh mint

1 cup chopped fresh cilantro

1 lime, cut into 4 to 6 wedges

## TO MAKE THE CURRY PASTE

In a food processor, blend the chiles, garlic, shallots, ginger, lime zest, coriander, peanut oil, and salt until pureed. Set aside or cover and refrigerate for up to 1 day.

## TO COOK THE CHICKEN

Season the chicken pieces with salt and pepper. Heat the oil in a large sauté pan over high heat. Add the seasoned chicken and brown on all sides, about 12 to 15 minutes. Transfer to a plate using a slotted spoon.

Add the mushrooms to the pan and cook for 1 minute over high heat. Stir the curry paste into the pan. Cook for 3 minutes, stirring frequently to prevent burning. Add the coconut milk, lime leaves, and lemongrass, and stir. Return the chicken pieces to the pan, lower the heat, and simmer, uncovered, for 20 minutes.

Remove the lime leaves and lemongrass, and serve the chicken and sauce in warmed bowls. Top each dish with the scallions, basil, mint, and cilantro, and add a lime wedge.

# roast chicken with fresh herbs, blood orange, and paprika

**SERVES 4**

With their deep red color and sweet taste, blood oranges offer an added dimension of color and flavor to this dish. This roast chicken is wonderful hot out of the oven, and any leftovers are even better the next day. Use it for chicken salad or shred it into your favorite soup. Use the bones for chicken stock so that nothing goes to waste.

**One 4-pound whole chicken**
**Salt and freshly ground pepper**
**2 blood, navel, or Valencia oranges, quartered**
**10 cloves garlic, smashed**
**1 small bunch thyme**
**1 tablespoon paprika**
**6 tablespoons salted butter, softened**
**4 to 6 sprigs parsley**

Preheat the oven to 450°F.

Rinse the chicken and pat dry. Set the chicken, breast side up, on a rack in a roasting pan. Season the inside of the cavity with salt and pepper. Squeeze one of the oranges all over, on the inside and outside of the chicken. Gently lift the skin of the breast and squeeze juice under the skin. Place the squeezed rinds inside the cavity. Put the garlic and ¾ of the thyme inside the cavity. Tie the legs together with kitchen twine. Season the outside of the chicken with salt, pepper, and paprika. Massage the butter under and over the chicken skin.

Roast the chicken for 10 minutes and then lower the oven temperature to 375°F for 50 to 60 minutes, or until the juices run clear—not pink—when the thigh is pierced with a knife. Remove from the oven and let rest for 15 minutes before carving.

Place the carved pieces on a platter and sprinkle with the parsley, remaining orange wedges, and remaining thyme.

# asian skewered peanut chicken thighs with asparagus

Chicken thighs absorb this flavorful marinade well and remain succulent after they've been cooked.

- 1 tablespoon grated orange zest
- ½ cup freshly squeezed orange juice
- 2 tablespoons peanut butter
- 1 tablespoon toasted sesame oil
- 4 cloves garlic, minced
- One 1-inch knob fresh ginger, peeled
- Pinch of salt
- Pinch of cayenne pepper
- 8 boneless, skinless chicken thighs
- 8 bamboo skewers
- 8 medium stalks asparagus, thick stalks trimmed, cut in half crosswise
- 1 tablespoon olive oil
- 1 tablespoon black sesame seeds (if tolerated), toasted (see page 53)
- 1 lemon, cut into 4 wedges

Place the zest, juice, peanut butter, sesame oil, garlic, ginger, salt, and cayenne in a food processor or blender and process until smooth.

Place the chicken thighs in a large resealable plastic bag, pour in the peanut butter mixture, and refrigerate for at least 1 hour or overnight.

Soak the skewers in water for at least 30 minutes.

Heat the grill to medium-high.

Rub the asparagus with the olive oil. Thread 1 piece of asparagus onto a skewer, then thread 1 piece of chicken, and then finish with another piece of asparagus. Repeat with the remaining skewers, asparagus, and chicken.

Grill for about 10 minutes on each side, or until the chicken is thoroughly cooked. If it begins to char before it is done, move the skewers to a cooler part of the grill.

Sprinkle the black sesame seeds on top and serve 2 skewers per person with a lemon wedge alongside.

# roast turkey breast with fresh herb sauce

This easy roast turkey breast recipe is quite versatile. It makes for a delicious dinner as well as great leftovers for sandwiches or salads. Try the lemon basil sauce on roasted vegetables as well.

> **4 pounds boneless turkey breast, tied**
> **Salt and freshly ground pepper**
> **4 cloves garlic**
> **1 tablespoon paprika**
> **1 tablespoon fresh marjoram**
> **1 tablespoon fresh oregano**
> **1 tablespoon fresh thyme**
> **1 tablespoon grated lemon zest**
> **8 tablespoons (1 stick) unsalted butter, softened**
> **Fresh Herb Sauce (recipe follows)**

Preheat the oven to 400°F.

Set the turkey on a rack in a roasting pan. Season with salt and pepper.

Place the garlic, paprika, marjoram, oregano, thyme, zest, and butter in a food processor and process until creamy and smooth. Rub this mixture all over the turkey.

Roast for 25 minutes, and then lower the oven temperature to 325°F. Roast, basting every 20 minutes, for 1 hour, or until the internal temperature of the turkey reaches 165°F.

Transfer to a cutting board and allow to rest for 10 minutes before slicing. Serve with the Fresh Herb Sauce drizzled on top.

# FRESH HERB SAUCE

MAKES 1½ CUPS

2 cups fresh herbs, such as basil, parsley, mint, marjoram, and thyme
2 cloves garlic
1 teaspoon grated lemon zest
½ cup freshly squeezed lemon juice (2 to 3 lemons)
¼ cup extra-virgin olive oil
Pinch of salt and freshly ground pepper

In a food processor or blender, puree the herbs, garlic, lemon zest, lemon juice, olive oil, salt, and pepper until smooth. Transfer to a serving bowl. This can be made 4 hours in advance and refrigerated. Bring to room temperature before serving.

# papaya-marinated grilled flank steak

SERVES 8 TO 10

In this dish the papaya not only lends a sweet flavor, but its fruit enzymes help break down any toughness in this flavorful cut of meat to create a truly tender flank steak. This is an easy dish to make for a crowd. Serve with Homemade Dijon Mustard (page 80).

**4 to 5 pounds flank steak**
**2 fresh papayas, peeled, seeded, and cut into chunks**
**¼ cup olive oil**
**7 cloves garlic, peeled**
**Salt and freshly ground pepper to taste**

Rinse the flank steak and pat dry. Set in a deep nonreactive baking pan. In a food processor or blender, puree the papayas, oil, garlic, salt, and pepper. Pour the mixture over the meat, cover, and place in the refrigerator for at least 24 hours or up to 3 days, which is preferable.

Preheat the grill to medium-high.

Remove the steak from the marinade and discard the marinade. Grill for about 5 minutes per side, depending on thickness, for medium rare. Transfer to a cutting board, cover with foil, and let rest for 10 minutes before slicing. Slice thinly against the grain.

# steak and vegetable stir-fry in lettuce cups

SERVES 4

This delicious Asian-inspired dish eaten on lettuce leaves makes for a fun and interesting presentation. Ginger, citrus, and cilantro combine here to lend a bright, clean flavor.

- 1 pound filet mignon, New York strip, or your favorite cut of steak, sliced very thin by your butcher
- Salt to taste
- Cayenne pepper to taste
- 2 tablespoons peanut oil
- 1 medium yellow onion, chopped
- 4 cloves garlic, minced
- One 1-inch knob fresh ginger, peeled and cut into thin matchsticks
- 4 ounces shiitake mushrooms, stems trimmed
- 1 tablespoon grated orange zest
- ½ cup freshly squeezed orange juice
- 4 ounces snow peas, strings removed
- 2 tablespoons toasted sesame oil
- ½ cup finely chopped fresh cilantro
- 1 head iceberg or romaine lettuce, separated into leaves

Season the beef with salt and cayenne. Heat a wok or large skillet over high heat. Add the peanut oil and beef. Brown for 2 minutes, stirring once or twice. Remove from the pan and set aside.

Add the onion, garlic, ginger, and mushrooms to the pan and cook over medium-high heat for 5 minutes. Add the zest and juice, and increase the heat to high again. Return the meat to the pan along with the snow peas and cook, stirring, for about 5 more minutes. Add more salt and cayenne if desired.

Remove from the heat and place in a serving bowl. Drizzle with the sesame oil and top with the cilantro. Serve the lettuce cups on the side. To eat, add a spoonful of the stir-fry to each lettuce cup and wrap the lettuce around the filling.

# ground beef chili with navy beans

SERVES 6 TO 8

This subtle twist on traditional chili is a crowd pleaser. Instead of using red beans, which aren't allowed on the diet, this chili uses navy beans, with great results. If you are symptom free, you may use black beans as well. It is best to make this chili one or two days ahead so that the flavors have a chance to develop. Reheat and serve with a simple green salad.

1½ cups navy beans

4 fresh Anaheim or poblano chiles

4 tablespoons olive oil

1½ pounds ground beef

Salt to taste

2 medium yellow onions, chopped

6 cloves garlic, chopped

¼ cup chile powder

2 bay leaves

2 teaspoons ground oregano

2 teaspoons ground cumin

1 teaspoon cayenne pepper

Two 14½-ounce cans Italian chopped tomatoes

4 tablespoons Italian tomato paste

½ cup red wine

Freshly ground pepper to taste

2 avocados, chopped

4 ounces cheddar cheese, grated (1 cup)

1 small red onion, chopped

1 cup Homemade Crème Fraîche (page 28)

Rinse and pick over the beans to remove any small pebbles, and then soak in water for 24 hours, changing the water halfway through. Rinse and drain.

Put the navy beans in a large pot, add fresh water to cover, and bring to a boil, skimming off any foam or empty bean skins from the surface. Lower the heat and cook at a low boil until tender, 1 to 1½ hours. Drain well.

Meanwhile, roast the chiles over an open flame or under a hot broiler until charred and black. Peel under cold running water and remove the seeds. Puree in a blender until smooth and set aside.

Heat 2 tablespoons oil in a large skillet. Add the beef, season with a pinch of salt, and brown about 10 minutes, stirring as needed. Set aside.

Heat the remaining 2 tablespoons oil in a large stockpot over medium-high heat. Add the onions and cook until translucent, about 3 minutes. Add the garlic and cook 1 more minute. Add the pureed chiles and cook for 30 seconds. Add the chile powder, bay leaves, oregano, cumin, and cayenne, and cook for 30 seconds to toast the spices. Add the chopped tomatoes, tomato paste, wine, and pepper, and stir. Add the beans, beef, and 1 cup water, and stir well. Cover and simmer for 30 minutes. Add more salt if desired.

Serve in warm bowls topped with avocado, cheddar cheese, red onion, and crème fraîche.

# kibbeh with yogurt and mint

SERVES 4

This Lebanese dish is traditionally made of seasoned ground beef stuffed into a pita-type bread or fried bulgur wheat shell. I love the spiced filling, but to make this recipe SCD compliant, I serve it in light, crunchy lettuce cups. Your guests and family will enjoy filling their own cups and topping them with tangy yogurt sauce.

3 tablespoons olive oil

2 pounds ground beef

1 medium yellow onion, chopped

4 cloves garlic, minced

2 tablespoons ground cumin

1½ teaspoons ground cinnamon

Pinch of ground cloves

Salt to taste

Cayenne pepper to taste

½ cup chopped fresh parsley

½ cup chopped fresh mint

1 cup roughly chopped walnuts

1 head iceberg lettuce, leaves separated

Cumin-Garlic Yogurt (recipe follows)

Heat 2 tablespoons oil in a large skillet over medium-high heat. Add the ground beef and brown it, breaking it up as it cooks, for about 5 minutes, or until cooked through. Remove from the pan and drain on paper towels.

Lower the heat and add the remaining tablespoon of oil to the pan. Add the onions and cook for about 3 minutes, or until translucent. Add the garlic and cook for 1 more minute. Add the cumin, cinnamon, cloves, salt, and cayenne, and cook for 1 more minute. Return the beef to the pan, stir well, and cook for 2 more minutes. Turn off the heat and stir in the parsley, mint, and walnuts.

Transfer the beef mixture to a pretty platter with a large spoon. Serve the lettuce cups and Cumin-Garlic Yogurt alongside. Scoop a spoonful of beef onto a lettuce leaf, top with yogurt, wrap, and eat.

# CUMIN-GARLIC YOGURT

1½ cups Homemade Yogurt (page 27)
2 cloves garlic, minced
1 tablespoon fresh mint, minced
1 teaspoon freshly grated lemon zest
1 tablespoon freshly squeezed lemon juice
1 tablespoon ground cumin
1 teaspoon paprika
½ teaspoon celery salt

In a medium bowl mix together the yogurt, garlic, mint, lemon zest and juice, cumin, paprika, and celery salt until well blended. This can be made up to 3 days in advance.

# baby back ribs with date-barbecue sauce

**SERVES 4**

These ribs are tender and sweet. The slow cooking process makes the meat just fall off the bones. The tangy sauce is a perfect complement. Serve with grilled apples, peaches, or pears.

**2 racks of baby back pork ribs (3 to 4 pounds)**
**Salt and freshly ground pepper**
**1 cup Date-Barbecue Sauce (recipe follows)**

Preheat the oven to 200° F.

Season the ribs with salt and pepper. Slather the barbecue sauce all over them and set them on a grill rack in a roasting pan. Place in the oven for 5 to 6 hours, until very tender.

Preheat the broiler.

Remove the ribs from the oven and broil for 30 seconds, until caramelized. Transfer to a cutting board, cut in between the ribs, and serve.

## DATE-BARBECUE SAUCE

**MAKES APPROXIMATELY 2 CUPS**

**1 tablespoon olive oil**
**½ small yellow onion, chopped**
**3 cloves garlic, minced**
**Pinch of cayenne pepper**
**1½ teaspoons Italian tomato paste**
**2 cups whole Italian tomatoes, pureed in a blender**
**½ cup red wine vinegar**
**2 tablespoons freshly squeezed orange juice**
**½ cup honey**
**1 tablespoon Homemade Dijon Mustard (page 80)**
**3 Medjool or Bohri dates, pitted and chopped**
**¾ teaspoon kosher salt, plus more to taste**
**1 teaspoon freshly ground pepper, plus more to taste**

Heat the oil in a medium saucepan over medium heat. Add the onion and cook until translucent and golden brown, about 5 minutes. Add the garlic and cayenne, and cook for 1 minute. Add the tomato paste and cook for another minute.

Add the tomatoes, vinegar, juice, honey, mustard, dates, salt, and pepper, and bring to a boil. Lower the heat and simmer for about 30 minutes, until thickened. Adjust the seasonings with salt and pepper.

Place in a food processor or blender in batches and process until smooth. Use right away or cool and store, covered, in the refrigerator for up to 5 days or in the freezer for up to 2 months.

# roast pork loin with stewed fruits

SERVES 4

This hearty autumn dish combines the subtle earthy flavors of apricots and prunes with the spirited kick of coriander, cardamom, and fennel.

**Two 1-pound pork tenderloins**
**Salt and freshly ground pepper**
**5 tablespoons olive oil**
**1 medium yellow onion, chopped**
**7 cloves garlic, chopped**
**1 bulb fennel, sliced**
**1 teaspoon ground coriander**
**1 teaspoon ground cardamom**
**1 teaspoon ground fennel**
**12 prunes**
**12 dried apricots**
**1 bunch thyme**
**1 cup red wine**
**2 tablespoons unsalted butter**

Preheat the oven to 400° F.

Season the pork with salt and pepper. Heat 2 tablespoons oil in a large skillet over medium-high heat. Add the pork and sear on all sides until golden brown, 7 to 10 minutes.

Coat the bottom of a large roasting pan with the remaining 3 tablespoons oil. Add the pork, onion, garlic, sliced fennel, coriander, cardamom, ground fennel, prunes, apricot, and thyme, and toss together until well mixed and the meat is well coated with oil and spices. Move the thyme under the meat. Roast for about 1 hour, or until the internal temperature of the meat is 140° F. Transfer the meat to a carving board and let rest for 15 minutes. Put the fruit and vegetables in a serving bowl and cover to keep warm. Discard the thyme.

To make the sauce, heat the roasting pan on top of the stove over high heat and add the red wine. Scrape up the bottom bits and boil for about 3 minutes, until reduced. Turn off the heat and stir in the butter. Adjust the seasoning with salt and pepper if needed. Transfer to a gravy boat.

Slice the meat on the diagonal. Serve with the roasted fruits and vegetables on the side and a little sauce on top.

# garlic and rosemary leg of lamb

SERVES 8

This is a wonderful springtime dish that is easy to make and excellent for leftovers. Cooked white navy beans (see page 84) are a great accompaniment for this.

**One 8-pound bone-in leg of lamb**
**Salt and freshly ground pepper**
**12 cloves garlic, peeled**
**3 tablespoons fresh rosemary**
**3 tablespoons olive oil**
**2 tablespoons Homemade Dijon Mustard (page 80)**
**Fresh Mint Sauce (page 76)**

Preheat the oven to 475° F.

Season the lamb with salt and pepper. Split 6 of the garlic cloves in half lengthwise. Stab the lamb all over with twelve 1-inch gashes and then fill the gashes with the split garlic halves.

In a food processor or blender, puree the remaining 6 cloves garlic, rosemary, oil, and mustard. Spread all over the lamb and then set the meat on a grill rack in a roasting pan.

Roast for 30 minutes. Lower the oven temperature to 350° F and cook for 1 hour, or until the internal temperature is 140° F for medium rare. Transfer to a cutting board and let rest for 30 minutes; the temperature will go up to about 145° F.

Slice thinly on the diagonal and serve with the mint sauce.

# shepherd's pie with mashed cauliflower

SERVES 4 TO 6

Shepherd's pie can be made with ground beef or ground lamb. I prefer the more intense flavor of lamb and add the mushrooms for their earthy texture and taste. Peas are also a standard ingredient, but I don't care for them in this dish. If you do, add ½ cup of fresh or frozen peas to it when you add the tomatoes.

3 tablespoons olive oil

2 pounds ground lamb

Salt and freshly ground pepper

2 onions, chopped

5 cloves garlic, chopped

4 ounces button or cremini mushrooms, chopped

One 8-ounce can whole tomatoes, chopped

1 tablespoon chopped fresh thyme

1 tablespoon grated lemon zest

½ cup chopped fresh parsley

1 medium head cauliflower, cut into florets

8 tablespoons (1 stick) butter

½ teaspoon freshly grated nutmeg

Preheat the oven to 400°F.

Heat 2 tablespoons oil in a large skillet over medium-high heat. Add the lamb, season with salt and pepper, and cook, stirring as needed, until browned, 12 to 15 minutes. Remove from the pan.

Heat the remaining tablespoon oil over medium heat and add the onion. Sauté until translucent, about 5 minutes. Add the garlic and cook for 1 minute. Add the mushrooms and cook for 4 minutes.

Return the lamb to the pan and add the tomatoes, thyme, and zest, and cook for 1 more minute. Turn off the heat and add the parsley, stirring thoroughly. Transfer the mixture to an 8- or 9-inch oval baking dish and set aside.

Meanwhile, in a steamer or in the bottom of a double boiler, bring an inch or so of water to a simmer over medium heat. Add the cauliflower to the steamer basket or the top of the double boiler, cover, and steam until tender, 8 to 10 minutes. In an electric mixer or food processor, or using a potato masher or ricer, mash the cauliflower with the butter and nutmeg until smooth. Spoon the cauliflower over the lamb. Bake in the oven for 20 minutes, until the top is lightly browned. Serve hot. (This can be made 4 hours in advance and refrigerated. Bring to room temperature before baking.)

# lamb keftas with yogurt dip

MAKES 12 TO 14 SKEWERS

Great as an hors d'oeuvre or a main course, these Moroccan ground lamb patties get a little sweetness from the pureed dates. Serve with Moroccan Cauliflower (page 149).

5 Medjool dates, pitted
1 small onion, quartered
2 cloves garlic
2 cups fresh parsley
2 cups fresh cilantro
2 cups fresh mint
8 ounces ground lamb
1 teaspoon ground cumin
1 teaspoon ground paprika
⅛ teaspoon salt
Cayenne pepper to taste
1½ cups Strained Homemade Yogurt (page 28)
12 to 14 bamboo skewers

Place the dates, onion, garlic, parsley, cilantro, and 1 cup mint in a food processor and process until finely chopped. Transfer to a bowl and mix in the lamb, cumin, paprika, salt, and cayenne by hand. Cover and chill in the refrigerator for at least 2 hours or overnight.

To make the dip, finely chop the remaining 1 cup mint and place in a medium bowl. Add the yogurt and mix together. Cover and chill until ready to serve or overnight.

Soak the bamboo skewers in water for at least 30 minutes.

Preheat the grill to medium.

Wrap the meat mixture around the skewers by mounding about a heaping tablespoon onto each skewer and then flattening the meat on two sides. Grill for 5 to 7 minutes on each side, until browned and cooked through. Serve while hot with the cold yogurt dip.

# vegetables

Grilled Portobello Mushroom Steaks Topped with No-Cook
   Tomato Sauce

Sorrel, Leek, and Zucchini Gratin

Zucchini Crespeu

Roasted Cipollini Onions with Thyme

Asparagus and Mushroom Frittata with Gouda Cheese and
   Tomato Chutney

Creamy Asparagus Puree

Mashed Peas with Mint

Grilled Scallions

Eggplant Charmoula

Mushroom Ratatouille

Oven-Dried Tomatoes

Braised Fennel in White Wine and Orange Juice with Thyme

Roasted Brussels Sprouts

Moroccan Cauliflower

Braised Purple Cabbage with Ground Caraway Seeds

Mashed Roasted Carrot with Cumin and Orange

Roasted Acorn Squash with Butter, Nutmeg, and Honey

**this chapter makes staying on the scd easy.** Fresh vegetables at the height of each season sometimes need nothing more than a quick toss in a pan with some olive oil, salt, and pepper. In other, more elaborate dishes, vegetables play the main role, such as Braised Purple Cabbage with Ground Caraway Seeds (page 150) and Mushroom Ratatouille (page 144).

The recipes in this chapter will tempt even the most vegetable-phobic people you know, including children! Interesting preparations and presentations also help encourage kids to eat vegetables. My kids dive into dishes like Sorrel, Leek, and Zucchini Gratin (page 135). It tastes so wonderful that they hardly realize they're consuming something good for them.

Note: Some people are not ready for fibrous vegetables such as cauliflower, broccoli, cabbage, fennel, and brussel sprouts, so go slowly and eat what you can tolerate. Usually the pea and the squash families are easier to start with.

# grilled portobello mushroom steaks topped with no-cook tomato sauce

SERVES 4

These mushrooms have the meaty consistency of steak and are fantastic smothered in this easy garlic sauce. To vary the recipe, substitute Spinach, Lemon, and Basil Pesto (page 75) or Carrot-Ginger Paste (page 78) for the sauce.

**TOMATO SAUCE**

1 pound fresh plum tomatoes, chopped

4 cloves garlic, minced

¼ cup fresh basil, cut into thin ribbons

½ cup extra-virgin olive oil

Salt and freshly ground pepper to taste

**MUSHROOMS**

4 large Portobello mushrooms, stems removed and caps brushed clean

3 tablespoons olive oil

Salt and freshly ground pepper to taste

## TO PREPARE THE SAUCE

In a medium bowl, stir together the tomatoes, garlic, basil, olive oil, salt, and pepper. Let sit at room temperature while you grill the mushrooms, or cover and refrigerate overnight.

## TO PREPARE THE MUSHROOMS

Preheat the grill to medium.

Rub the mushrooms with oil, salt, and pepper. Grill for 8 to 10 minutes. Turn over and grill for another 15 minutes, or until golden brown.

Top each mushroom, underside facing up, with tomato sauce and serve.

# sorrel, leek, and zucchini gratin

SERVES 10 TO 12 AS A SIDE DISH

This sumptuous and savory summer treat is perfect as a side dish or a vegetarian main course. You can make it in individual ramekins as well (by cooking for 15 to 20 minutes, until golden brown on top).

4 tablespoons olive oil

2 tablespoons unsalted butter

4 medium leeks, white and green parts, thinly sliced

Salt and freshly ground pepper to taste

4 medium shallots, chopped

2 cups chopped sorrel leaves

1 tablespoon fresh thyme leaves

3 medium zucchini, thinly sliced

8 ounces Gruyère cheese, grated (2 cups)

Preheat the oven to 375° F. Butter an 8 × 8-inch baking or gratin dish.

Heat a large sauté pan over medium-high heat. Add 2 tablespoons oil, butter, and leeks. Cook the leeks until translucent, about 5 minutes. Season with salt and pepper. Lower the heat to medium and add the shallots, sorrel, and thyme. Cook for 3 more minutes. Remove from the heat and set aside.

Layer the bottom of the gratin dish with half of the zucchini slices. Drizzle with about 2 teaspoons oil and sprinkle with salt and pepper. Top with a layer of the leek mixture, spreading it evenly. Repeat with both the zucchini and the leek mixture. Spread the Gruyère on top and set the dish in the oven. Cook for 30 minutes, or until golden. Serve immediately.

# zucchini crespeu

This lovely luncheon dish, a frittata of sorts, hails from the south of France. Serve it with Homemade Dijon Mustard (page 80) and a glass of dry white wine. This recipe also makes a nice light dinner or an accompaniment for soup.

2 medium zucchini

1 tablespoon olive oil

2 tablespoons fresh marjoram or thyme, plus a few sprigs for garnish

2 garlic cloves, chopped

9 large eggs, beaten

Salt and freshly ground pepper to taste

¾ cup grated Parmesan cheese, or more to taste

Preheat the broiler.

Shred the zucchini in a food processor or on the large holes of a box grater. Squeeze out all the liquid.

Heat the oil in a 12-inch ovenproof skillet over medium heat. Add the zucchini and cook for 3 to 4 minutes, until just tender. Add the marjoram and garlic, and cook for about 1 minute.

Pour in the eggs and season with salt and pepper. Tilt the pan so that the eggs spread out. Lift the cooked eggs in parts with a spatula and let the uncooked egg flow underneath. Cook for 1 minute. Sprinkle the Parmesan cheese on top and place the pan under the broiler until the cheese browns slightly, about 5 minutes.

Slide the crespeu onto a pretty plate and serve garnished with a few sprigs of fresh marjoram.

# roasted cipollini onions with thyme

These squat little onions are succulent and sweet. A little butter, thyme, and garlic are all that is needed to bring out their best. If you can't find cipollini onions, you can substitute pearl onions.

> 12 medium-sized cipollini onions, outer layer of skin removed
> 2 tablespoons olive oil
> 4 cloves garlic, minced
> 2 tablespoons fresh thyme
> 4 tablespoons butter, cut into pieces
> Salt and freshly ground pepper to taste

Preheat the oven to 400°F.

Peel the onions and cut off the bottoms so they stand up without wobbling. Cut an X into the tops of each onion with a sharp knife. Rub the onions with oil and set in a baking dish. Put garlic into the cut at the top of each onion and then add some thyme and butter. Season with salt and pepper. Roast for 45 minutes, until golden brown and tender. Serve warm.

# asparagus and mushroom frittata with gouda cheese and tomato chutney

SERVES 4

This dish is very versatile. It can be served for breakfast, lunch, or dinner. The tomato chutney is also wonderful alongside grilled or roasted meat and fish, and it can be spread on sandwiches.

**8 large eggs**

**Salt and freshly ground pepper**

**3 tablespoons unsalted butter**

**2 tablespoons olive oil**

**4 ounces cremini or button mushrooms, cleaned and chopped**

**6 medium stalks asparagus, chopped**

**4 ounces Gouda cheese, grated (1 cup)**

**Tomato Chutney (recipe follows)**

Preheat the broiler.

Beat the eggs with 1 tablespoon water and salt and pepper to taste. Set aside.

In a large ovenproof sauté pan over medium heat, melt 2 tablespoons butter with 1 tablespoon oil. Add the mushrooms and cook until golden brown, about 5 minutes. Add the asparagus and cook for 2 more minutes.

Add the remaining tablespoon butter and the remaining tablespoon oil, and stir to incorporate. Pour in the eggs, tilting the pan to spread them out evenly. Lift the cooked parts up with a spatula to allow the uncooked eggs to slide under. Cook for 1 minute. Sprinkle the Gouda cheese on top and place the pan under the broiler for 2 minutes, or until bubbly and puffy.

Cut in sections and serve with tomato chutney.

# TOMATO CHUTNEY

MAKES 2 CUPS

1 tablespoon olive oil

½ small yellow onion, chopped

2 cloves garlic, minced

3 teaspoons grated fresh ginger

3 plum tomatoes, peeled, seeded, and chopped

1 cup raisins

1 apple, peeled, cored, and chopped

1 cup apple cider vinegar

1 cup honey

2 Medjool dates, minced

Salt and freshly ground pepper

Heat the oil in a large saucepan over medium heat. Add the onion and cook until translucent, about 5 minutes. Add the garlic and ginger, and cook for 1 minute. Add the tomatoes, raisins, apple, vinegar, honey, and dates. Season with salt and pepper. Lower the heat and simmer, stirring occasionally, for about 1 hour, until thick. Remove from the heat and set aside to cool. Store in a container with a tight-fitting lid in the refrigerator for up to 1 week.

# creamy asparagus puree

Try making this delicious dish in springtime when asparagus is at its peak of flavor. In autumn, substitute carrots, broccoli, cauliflower, butternut squash, or uncooked spinach or watercress for the asparagus.

**1 pound medium asparagus, roughly chopped**

**4 ounces (½ cup) farmer cheese**

**¼ cup freshly grated Parmesan cheese**

**1/4 cup Basic Chicken Stock (page 55) or Roasted Vegetable Stock (page 56)**

**1 clove garlic, chopped**

**Salt and freshly ground black pepper to taste**

In a steamer or the bottom of a double boiler, bring an inch or so of water to a simmer over medium heat. Add the asparagus to the steamer basket or the top of the double boiler, cover, and steam the asparagus until tender, about 7 minutes.

Meanwhile, place the farmer and Parmesan cheeses, broth, garlic, salt, and pepper in a food processor and process until well mixed. Add the asparagus and process again until smooth. Adjust the seasonings and serve hot.

# mashed peas with mint

This traditional English dish goes well with roasted meats and is a wonderful substitute for mashed potatoes. The vibrant green color is as intense as the flavor.

6 cups shelled fresh peas (6 to 6½ pounds in the pod) or one 1-pound
  package frozen peas
1 tablespoon unsalted butter
2 tablespoons extra-virgin olive oil
2 cloves garlic
1 tablespoon grated lemon zest
¼ cup freshly squeezed lemon juice (1 to 2 lemons)
½ cup fresh mint leaves
Salt and freshly ground pepper to taste

Place the peas, butter, and enough water to cover in a medium saucepan. Cover and bring to a simmer for about 15 minutes (5 minutes if using frozen peas), until tender.

Meanwhile, put the oil, garlic, cloves, zest, juice, and mint leaves in a food processor and process until smooth. Drain the peas, add them to the food processor with salt and pepper, and pulse until creamy but chunky. Serve immediately.

# grilled scallions

So simple, so easy, and so delicious! These scallions can be served as a side dish or as part of a vegetable platter with Artichoke Dip (page 86).

**2 tablespoons olive oil**
**20 scallions, roots trimmed**
**Salt and freshly ground pepper**
**Balsamic vinegar for serving**

Preheat the grill to medium.

Rub the oil over all the scallions and season them with salt and pepper. Place the scallions perpendicular to the grates of the grill. Cook for about 10 minutes, until slightly charred and tender. Roll the scallions often to avoid burning.

Serve on a platter, either hot or at room temperature, drizzled with balsamic vinegar. Peel off charred skin and eat.

# eggplant charmoula

SERVES 8 TO 10

This is a wonderful, simple Moroccan eggplant dish that I have been making since long before I discovered the SCD. Salting the eggplant removes any bitterness. Serve with Lamb Keftas with Yogurt Dip (page 130).

2 large eggplants
½ cup salt
1 cup olive oil
6 cloves garlic, minced
1 tablespoon ground cumin
1 tablespoon paprika
¼ cup chopped flat-leaf parsley

Slice the eggplants into ¼-inch rounds. Lay them out in a single layer on paper towels and generously salt both sides. Place 2 layers of paper towels on top and gently press down with your hands. Set aside for 30 minutes and then change the paper towels, pressing down again. Let sit for another 30 minutes.

Mix the oil, garlic, cumin, and paprika in a measuring cup with a spout.

Rinse all the salt from the eggplant slices under running water and pat them dry. Arrange in a nonreactive shallow baking dish and pour the oil mixture on top. Refrigerate for at least 1 hour or overnight.

Drain the excess oil from the eggplant slices into a large skillet set over medium heat. Add the eggplant slices, working in batches, and cook for about 5 minutes per side, until lightly browned. Remove and drain on paper towels. Repeat with the remaining eggplant slices.

Place on a serving plate and sprinkle with the parsley. Serve hot or at room temperature.

# mushroom ratatouille

SERVES 10

This ratatouille is a great way to use up an abundance of end-of-season vegetables. It makes a great accompaniment to grilled meats. Try leftovers in an
omelet or add them to your favorite sandwich.

1 large eggplant, sliced into ½-inch rounds
Salt
½ cup olive oil
2 cups (8 ounces) cremini or button mushrooms
2 large zucchini, sliced into ½-inch rounds
2 large yellow summer squash, sliced into ½-inch rounds
4 medium yellow onions, chopped
12 cloves garlic, chopped
1 tablespoon fresh thyme leaves
2 red bell peppers, chopped
2 green bell peppers, chopped
6 medium tomatoes, peeled, seeded, and chopped
1 tablespoon fresh oregano leaves (optional)
1 tablespoon fresh marjoram leaves (optional)
1 tablespoon fresh tarragon leaves (optional)
Freshly ground pepper
¼ cup extra-virgin olive oil
1 cup fresh basil leaves, cut into thin ribbons

Lay the eggplant slices in a single layer on paper towels and generously salt both sides.
Place 2 layers of paper towels on top and gently press down with your hands. Set aside
for 30 minutes and then change the paper towels, pressing down again. Let sit for another
30 minutes. Cut into small chunks.

Heat ¼ cup olive oil in a large pot over medium-high heat. Add the eggplant and cook,
stirring occasionally, until golden brown. Remove the eggplant with a slotted spoon and
set aside on a large plate.

Add 2 tablespoons olive oil to the pot along with the mushrooms. Cook until golden brown, about 7 to 9 minutes. Remove with a slotted spoon and set aside with the eggplant.

Add 1 tablespoon olive oil to the pot along with the zucchini and squash. Cook until golden brown, about 7 minutes. Remove with a slotted spoon and set aside with the eggplant.

Add the remaining tablespoon of olive oil to the pot along with the onions. Cook for 5 minutes, until translucent. Add the garlic and thyme, and cook for 1 more minute. Add the red and green bell peppers, tomatoes, oregano, marjoram, and tarragon. Season with salt and pepper. Stir well and cook for about 10 minutes on high.

Return the reserved vegetables to the pan and simmer over medium-low heat, covered, for about 30 minutes. This can be made up to 1 day in advance and kept covered in the refrigerator.

Serve warm, at room temperature, or chilled. Drizzle with extra-virgin olive oil and sprinkle with basil.

# oven-dried tomatoes

MAKES 50 TO 60 SLICES

Slow roasting at a low temperature helps concentrate the flavors of tomatoes even when they are out of season. Serve these right out of the oven as a side dish or let them cool and store them in a jar with ½ cup of extra-virgin olive oil. They will keep refrigerated for up to two weeks and are great in salads and sandwiches.

**10 plum tomatoes, cut into ½-inch slices**
**3 tablespoons olive oil**
**Salt and freshly ground pepper to taste**

Preheat the oven to 200° F.

Lay out the tomatoes on 2 parchment-covered rimmed baking sheets. Drizzle with the oil and sprinkle with salt and pepper.

Place in the oven for 4 to 5 hours, until dried. The longer you cook them, the drier they will be. Serve warm, at room temperature, or chilled.

# braised fennel in white wine and orange juice with thyme

SERVES 6

The anise flavor of fennel combines perfectly with sweet-tart orange juice
and fragrant thyme in this perfect winter vegetable dish.

3 medium fennel bulbs, trimmed, halved, and fronds reserved

3 tablespoons olive oil

Salt and freshly ground pepper to taste

¼ cup dry white wine

5 cloves garlic, chopped

¾ cup freshly squeezed orange juice (1 to 2 oranges)

1 tablespoon fresh thyme

Rub the fennel halves with 2 tablespoons oil and season with salt and pepper.

Heat the remaining tablespoon oil in a large skillet over high heat. Add the fennel
halves, cut side down, and cook for about 5 minutes, or until golden brown. Turn and cook
the other side for about 3 minutes. Pour in the wine, bring to a boil, and cook for 30 seconds. Add the garlic, juice, and thyme. Bring everything to a boil, then lower the heat to
medium-low and cover the pan. Simmer for 10 minutes, until the fennel is nearly tender.

Uncover and cook over medium-high heat until the juices have reduced and the fennel
is tender, about 10 minutes.

Serve hot, sprinkled with the reserved fennel fronds.

# roasted brussels sprouts

**SERVES 4 TO 6**

Roasting brussels sprouts at high heat caramelizes them and helps bring out their natural sweetness. I like to add a little orange zest and cumin for extra flavor. Serve with Garlic and Rosemary Leg of Lamb (page 127).

**1 pound brussels sprouts, trimmed and outer tough leaves removed**
**2 tablespoons olive oil**
**1 tablespoon grated orange zest**
**1 tablespoon ground cumin**
**Salt and freshly ground pepper to taste**

Preheat the oven to 425° F.

In a medium bowl toss together the brussels sprouts, olive oil, zest, cumin, salt, and pepper. Transfer to a baking dish or a rimmed baking sheet. Roast for 15 to 20 minutes, or until golden brown and tender. Serve hot.

# moroccan cauliflower

SERVES 4 TO 6

The deep red color of paprika seeps into the cauliflower, which is kept whole, making for a beautiful presentation. The cumin and cinnamon add wonderful flavor to this vegetable side dish. This is great alongside Moroccan Chicken Stew with Cashews, Saffron, and Currants (page 110).

1 medium head cauliflower

1 teaspoon paprika

1 teaspoon ground cumin

$\frac{1}{8}$ teaspoon ground cinnamon

$\frac{1}{4}$ cup extra-virgin olive oil

2 tablespoons freshly squeezed lemon juice

2 cloves garlic, minced

1 teaspoon salt

1 teaspoon freshly ground pepper

$\frac{1}{3}$ cup chopped flat-leaf parsley

Trim the stalk of the cauliflower to the base, keeping the pretty green leaves intact. Set in a large pot with half an inch of water in it. Cover, set over medium heat, and bring to a simmer. Steam until tender, 10 to 12 minutes.

Meanwhile, in a small sauté pan over medium-low heat, lightly toast the paprika, cumin, and cinnamon for 2 to 4 minutes, until fragrant. Remove from the heat and whisk in the oil, juice, garlic, salt, and pepper.

Transfer the cauliflower to a platter and pour the spiced oil over the top. Sprinkle with the parsley and serve.

# braised purple cabbage with ground caraway seeds

Serve this beautiful purple cabbage, sautéed with citrus and butter, with Roast Pork Loin with Stewed Fruits (page 126). If you are tolerating seeds well at this point, you do not need to grind them after toasting.

- 1 tablespoon caraway seeds
- 2 tablespoons unsalted butter
- 1 tablespoon olive oil
- 3 cloves garlic, chopped
- 1 medium head purple cabbage, cored and sliced into ½-inch pieces
- 1 teaspoon grated orange zest
- ½ cup freshly squeezed orange juice (about 2 oranges)
- Salt and freshly ground pepper to taste

Toast the caraway seeds in a dry skillet over medium heat until fragrant, about 3 minutes. Let cool, then grind to a powder in a spice mill and set aside.

Heat a large, deep sauté pan over medium heat. Add the butter, oil, and garlic, and cook for 1 minute, taking care not to brown the garlic. Add the caraway seeds and stir. Add the cabbage, zest, juice, salt, pepper, and ½ cup water. Stir, then cover, lower the heat, and simmer for 40 minutes. Serve hot. This can be stored in a covered container in the refrigerator for up to 3 days.

# mashed roasted carrot with cumin and orange

SERVES 4

This deep, rich orange puree is a great substitute for mashed potatoes and, if you ask me, has even more flavor. The roasted garlic butter adds even more rich, sweet flavor. Serve with a variety of Moroccan or Middle Eastern–inspired dishes.

**2 pounds carrots, peeled, trimmed, and cut into 2-inch pieces**
**8 cloves garlic, unpeeled**
**¼ cup olive oil**
**2 teaspoons ground cumin**
**1 tablespoon grated orange zest**
**Salt and freshly ground pepper to taste**
**3 tablespoons unsalted butter**

Preheat the oven to 400° F.

In a roasting pan, toss the carrots with the garlic, oil, cumin, zest, salt, and pepper. Roast for 1 hour, until very tender. Drain any excess oil from the carrots and transfer them to a food processor. Squeeze the garlic out of its skin into the food processor and add 1 tablespoon butter. Pulse to a chunky puree. This can be made 2 days in advance and stored in a covered container in the refrigerator.

Cut the remaining 2 tablespoons butter into 6 slices and top each serving with a slice.

# roasted acorn squash with butter, nutmeg, and honey

SERVES 4

These exquisite little squash boats are so sweet and good that they are almost like a dessert. They are perfect to serve at Thanksgiving and Christmas.

2 medium acorn squash, cut in half crosswise and seeds removed
2 tablespoons olive oil
2 tablespoons unsalted butter, cut into 4 pieces
¼ teaspoon freshly grated nutmeg
1 teaspoon grated orange zest
Sea salt and freshly ground pepper to taste
¼ cup honey

Preheat the oven to 400° F.

Cut the ends off each squash so they sit flat without wobbling. Set on a cookie sheet, scooped-out side up. Rub oil on the flesh of each half and divide the butter among the cavities. Sprinkle with the nutmeg, zest, salt, and pepper. Roast for 45 minutes, until tender when poked with a fork. Drizzle honey on top and cook for 10 more minutes. Serve hot.

# mock starches

Lime and Sea Salt Tortilla Chips

Havarti Dill Quesadillas

Buttery Herb and Garlic Crackers

Cashew Bread

Pulsed Cashew Couscous

Gougères

Oven-Roasted Butternut Squash Fries

Butternut Squash Chips

Celery Root Mashed Potatoes

Spaghetti Squash with Puttanesca Sauce

Pasta Aglio Oglio with Enoki Mushrooms

Zucchini Lasagna

Pizza Margherita

Falafel with Navy Beans

**these mock starches are healthy substitutes** for real starches, which are not allowed on the SCD eating plan. They are made from vegetables, eggs, or nuts but perform and often taste just like a "real" starch. You won't miss the heavy, bloated feeling that real starches give you. And for those of you who have been sick, you won't miss the pain!

Kids and adults both love Havarti Dill Quesadillas (page 158), and you'll never miss conventional bread once you try Cashew Bread (page 160), which is excellent sliced, either fresh or toasted, for sandwiches. If you crave potato chips, try Oven-Roasted Butternut Squash Fries (page 163) and Lime and Sea Salt Tortilla Chips (page 156). You'll never long for traditional heavy mashed potatoes again after you try Celery Root Mashed Potatoes (page 165). And if pasta is your weakness, turn to Pasta Aglio Oglio with Enoki Mushrooms (page 167).

These creative healthy replacements for traditional starches can be used in several ways: as a base for sauces and other flavorings, as accompaniments to entrées, and as a tasty snack. Go ahead and indulge, because they are absolutely legal.

# lime and sea salt tortilla chips

MAKES 32 CHIPS

These oven-baked chips are delicious on their own or served with Mango-Currant Chutney (page 37). If you have a dehydrator, you can set it to 120°F and dry the chips in it for eight hours.

**8 Cashew Butter Tortillas (recipe follows)**
**¼ cup freshly squeezed lime juice (2 to 3 limes)**
**Salt**

Preheat the oven to 200°F.

Cut each tortilla into 4 triangles. Brush on both sides with the juice and sprinkle with salt. Lay the chips on parchment paper–lined baking sheets and bake for 6 hours, until crisp. Remove from the oven and let cool. Store in an airtight container for up to 3 days.

## middle eastern pita chips

Mix the following with the lime juice: ¼ cup olive oil, 4 cloves minced garlic, 1 tablespoon ground cumin, and 1 tablespoon paprika. Proceed as for Lime and Sea Salt Tortilla Chips. Serve with White Bean Hummus (page 84) or Yogurt Curry Dip (page 83).

# CASHEW BUTTER TORTILLAS

**MAKES ABOUT TWENTY 5-INCH TORTILLAS**
You will need a tortilla iron to make these delicious tortillas.


**3 cups unsalted cashew butter**

**4 large eggs**

**2 tablespoons freshly squeezed lime juice (about 1 lime)**

**4 tablespoons unsalted butter, melted**

**1 teaspoon kosher salt**

**½ teaspoon baking soda**


Preheat a tortilla iron following the manufacturer's directions.

In a food processor puree the cashew butter, eggs, lime juice, butter, salt, and baking soda until smooth.

Drop a large spoonful of batter onto the hot iron and cook according to the manufacturer's directions. Lay the cooked tortillas on paper towels to cool, placing a paper towel between the tortillas so they won't stick to each other. Store in a plastic bag in the refrigerator for up to 2 weeks or in the freezer for up to 6 months.

# havarti dill quesadillas

SERVES 4 TO 6

These delicious quesadillas are good with salsa, guacamole, or Mango-Currant Chutney (page 37).

**4 tablespoons unsalted butter**

**4 teaspoons olive oil**

**8 Cashew Butter Tortillas (page 157)**

**8 ounces Havarti cheese, grated (2 cups)**

**1 teaspoon chopped fresh dill**

Preheat the oven to 200° F.

Heat 1 tablespoon butter and 1 teaspoon oil in a medium skillet over medium heat. Add 1 tortilla to the pan and sprinkle with ½ cup cheese and a pinch of dill. Lay another tortilla on top and press down gently. Cook for a couple of minutes, until golden brown. Flip and cook the other side for 2 more minutes, or until the cheese has melted and the quesadillas are golden brown. Transfer to a baking sheet and put in the oven to keep warm while you make 3 more quesadillas.

Cut each quesadilla into 4 wedges and serve hot.

# buttery herb and garlic crackers

MAKES ABOUT 20
These are so good and crunchy. Try substituting your own favorite spice combinations for the herbs. If you have a dehydrator, set it to 150°F and dry the crackers in it for eight hours.

1 loaf Cashew Bread (page 160), thinly sliced
8 tablespoons unsalted butter (1 stick), melted
3 cloves garlic, minced
1 teaspoon dried Italian herbs (a mix of oregano, basil, parsley, and
   rosemary)
Salt to taste

Preheat the oven to 200°F.

Lay the bread slices on baking sheets. In a bowl, mix the butter with the garlic, herbs, and salt. Using a pastry brush, evenly coat both sides of the bread slices with the butter mixture. Bake for 8 hours, until crisp. Remove from the oven and let cool. Keep in a sealable plastic bag for up to 3 days.

# cashew bread

I like to make three loaves of this delicious bread at once, because we go through it so fast in my house. If you don't have three loaf pans, the recipe can be scaled down easily. When sliced, this bread is excellent as toast and for sandwiches.

6 large eggs, separated
1 teaspoon salt
6 cups unsalted raw cashews
1 tablespoon apple cider vinegar
2 cups Homemade Yogurt (page 27)
1 cup apple juice
1½ teaspoons baking soda

Preheat the oven to 300°F.

Line three 8½ × 4½-inch loaf pans with parchment paper and place on a baking sheet. Set aside.

Using an electric mixer on medium speed, beat the egg whites with the salt until stiff peaks form.

Meanwhile, grind the cashews in a food processor until as smooth as possible. With the motor running, add the vinegar, yogurt, juice, egg yolks, and baking soda. Blend well and then transfer to a large bowl. Gently fold half of the egg whites into the cashew mixture to lighten the batter, then fold in the rest until combined.

Pour the batter into loaf pans and bake for 1 hour and 15 minutes, until a knife inserted in the center of each cake comes out clean. Cool for 15 minutes, then remove from the pans and cool completely on a rack.

Well wrapped, the loaves will keep for 2 days at room temperature, 5 days in the refrigerator, and up to 2 months in the freezer.

Spinach Salad with Crispy Prosciutto, Poached Eggs, and Caramelized Onions, p. 46

ABOVE Mexican Black Bean Soup, p. 59

OPPOSITE French Three-Onion Soup with Gruyère, p. 57

ABOVE Chilled Pea Soup, p. 68
OPPOSITE Fresh Spring Rolls with Spicy Chile Dipping Sauce, p. 34

ABOVE Havarti Dill Quesadillas, p. 158, with Mango-Currant Chutney, p. 37
OPPOSITE Fresh Shaved Beet Salad with Fresh Mint and Herbed Farmer Cheese, p. 44

ABOVE Skewered Shrimps in Mint Pesto, p. 39

OPPOSITE Banana Leaf–Wrapped Halibut with Papaya and Coconut, p. 100

ABOVE Seared Ahi Tuna Tartare with Sesame, Avocado, and Ginger, p. 104
BELOW Asian Skewered Peanut Chicken Thighs with Asparagus, p. 115
OPPOSITE Moroccan Cauliflower, p. 149

ABOVE *(clockwise, from left)* Yogurt Curry Dip, p. 83, Roasted Red Pepper Spread, p. 79, White Bean Hummus, p. 84

OPPOSITE Garlic and Rosemary Leg of Lamb, p. 127, with Fresh Mint Sauce, p. 76

ABOVE Tarte Tatin, p. 178
OPPOSITE Roasted Acorn Squash with Butter, Nutmeg, and Honey, p. 152

ABOVE Pecan Waffles with Sautéed Bananas and Cinnamon Honey, p. 208
BELOW Lemon-Coconut Macaroons, p. 176

# pulsed cashew couscous

SERVES 4

When finely chopped in a food processor, cashews become couscous-like, only crunchier and nuttier. These are a great accompaniment to a good stew or thick sauce. Try adding a little lemon juice, minced garlic, and some olive oil for extra flavor if desired.

**2 cups unsalted raw cashews**
**1 teaspoon salt**

Pulse the nuts with the salt in a food processor until small and couscous-like. Be careful not to overpulse them, or you'll end up with cashew butter.

# gougères

These delicate puffed cheese balls make excellent hors d'oeuvres and snacks. Kids love them, too.

1 cup cashews
½ cup Homemade Yogurt (page 27)
4 tablespoons butter
Pinch of freshly grated nutmeg
Pinch of salt
Pinch of cayenne pepper
3 large eggs
¼ cup grated Parmesan cheese
¼ cup grated Gruyère cheese

Preheat the oven to 425° F. Line a large baking sheet with parchment paper.

In a food processor, grind the cashews as finely as possible. Set aside.

In a small saucepan over medium heat, heat the yogurt, butter, nutmeg, salt, and cayenne until scalded. Add the cashews all at once and stir vigorously with a wooden spoon until the mixture is incorporated. Cook and stir continuously for 1½ more minutes, until the mixture pulls away from the sides of the pan. Pour into the food processor and add 2 of the eggs, the Parmesan, and the Gruyère. Mix until smooth.

Drop in spoonfuls about the size of a golf ball on the baking sheet. Beat the remaining egg with 1 teaspoon water and brush the mounds with the egg wash. Bake for 12 minutes, or until golden brown; serve hot.

# oven-roasted butternut squash fries

SERVES 4

These are a great and healthy substitute for fries made from potatoes. Choose your favorite dip to go along with them. White Bean Hummus (page 84), Lucques Olive Tapenade (page 87), Yogurt Curry Dip (page 83), and Roasted Red Pepper Spread (page 79) are all good. You can also flavor them by stirring any of the following into the olive oil: minced garlic, ground cumin, dried Italian herbs, finely chopped fresh dill, cayenne pepper, or finely chopped fresh parsley.

**1 large butternut squash (about 2 pounds)**
**¼ cup olive oil**
**Salt to taste**

Preheat the oven to 425° F.

Peel the squash, then split it in half and remove the seeds. Cut into wedges about 4 inches long and ½ inch wide.

Toss the squash with the oil and salt on a baking sheet. Bake for 40 to 45 minutes, until tender and lightly brown. Use a spatula to turn the fries every 10 minutes or so to prevent burning. Serve hot.

# butternut squash chips

Delicious, crunchy, and salty, these are a great substitute for unhealthy regular potato chips. They hit the spot!

**Vegetable or coconut oil**
**1 small butternut squash, long "neck" portion only, peeled (reserve the
    bulb portion for another use)**
**Salt to taste**

In a large, wide frying pan or shallow pot over medium heat, heat 1 inch of oil to 350°F as measured on a deep-fry thermometer.

Meanwhile, using a mandoline or sharp knife, slice the squash into thin rounds, about $\frac{1}{16}$ inch thick. Place a few in the oil and fry for $1\frac{1}{2}$ to 2 minutes, until golden brown on both sides. Remove with a slotted spoon and drain on paper towels. Repeat with the remaining squash slices. Season with salt and serve.

# celery root mashed potatoes

SERVES 6

Creamy, thick, and satisfying, mashed celery root is a great substitute for potatoes. Serve with Roast Chicken with Fresh Herbs, Blood Orange, and Paprika (page 114).

**2 pounds celery root, peeled and chopped**

**3 tablespoons olive oil**

**Salt and freshly ground pepper to taste**

**4 tablespoons unsalted butter**

**3 tablespoons snipped fresh chives**

Preheat the oven to 425° F.

Toss the celery root with the oil, salt, and pepper in a roasting pan. Roast for 25 to 30 minutes, or until tender.

Transfer to a warm bowl and mash with a potato masher, then press through a ricer. Stir in the butter. Sprinkle the chives on top and serve.

This can be made ahead, cooled, covered, and refrigerated overnight. Reheat, covered, in a 250° F oven until hot.

# spaghetti squash with puttanesca sauce

SERVES 4 TO 6

No other vegetable so closely resembles a starch. After cooking, the strands of squash come out looking just like spaghetti noodles. Better still, this vegetable can stand up to any sauce. Instead of Puttanesca Sauce, try it with Spinach, Lemon, and Basil Pesto (page 75) or Classic Tomato Sauce (page 74).

1 large spaghetti squash (3½ to 4 pounds)
3 tablespoons olive oil
Salt and freshly ground pepper to taste
½ teaspoon red pepper flakes
5 cloves garlic, chopped
10 plum tomatoes, peeled, seeded, and chopped
2 tablespoons drained capers
½ cup pitted Kalamata olives
2 tablespoons unsalted butter
10 fresh basil leaves, cut into thin ribbons
¼ cup freshly grated Parmesan cheese

Preheat the oven to 425°F.

Cut the spaghetti squash in half lengthwise and remove the seeds. Rub the squash with 1 tablespoon oil and sprinkle with salt and pepper. Place on a baking sheet, cut side up, and roast for 45 to 60 minutes, or until tender.

Meanwhile, heat the remaining 2 tablespoons oil in a large skillet over medium heat. Add the red pepper flakes and garlic, and sauté for 1 minute, taking care not to brown the garlic. Add the tomatoes, capers, and olives, and simmer gently over low heat for 30 minutes.

Turn off the heat, swirl in the butter, and stir in the basil.

Run a fork over the spaghetti squash to separate it into strands. Place the squash on a serving platter or divide among individual bowls. Pour the sauce on top, sprinkle with the Parmesan, and serve.

# pasta aglio oglio with enoki mushrooms

SERVES 4 AS A SIDE DISH

This dish—where long, thin white enoki mushrooms take the place of pasta in a simple, spicy garlic and olive oil sauce—is truly a delicacy and much more delicious than regular pasta. You can usually find enoki mushrooms in large, well-stocked supermarkets or Asian specialty shops. To serve this as a main course, double the recipe.

4 tablespoons olive oil

Four 3½-ounce packages enoki mushrooms, rinsed, drained, and ends trimmed

4 cloves garlic, chopped

1 teaspoon red pepper flakes

1 tablespoon finely chopped fresh flat-leaf parsley

Salt and freshly ground pepper to taste

Freshly grated Parmesan cheese to taste

Heat the oil in a medium skillet over medium heat. Add the mushrooms, garlic, and pepper flakes, and cook for a few minutes, until the mushrooms are just tender. Stir often and be careful not to let the garlic burn.

Turn off the heat. Add the parsley, salt, pepper, and Parmesan, toss, and serve.

# zucchini lasagna

SERVES 4 TO 6

Thinly sliced zucchini works well instead of pasta sheets in this delicious lasagna. I use a mix of three dry cheeses for extra flavor. Try experimenting with different additions such as sautéed mushrooms, sliced olives, capers, bell peppers, prosciutto, or sautéed ground beef or chicken.

**2 medium zucchini, peeled**
**1 cup Classic Tomato Sauce (page 74)**
**¼ cup olive oil**
**4 ounces farmer cheese, crumbled (1 cup)**
**3 ounces Asiago cheese, grated (about 1 cup)**
**4 ounces Monterey Jack cheese, grated (1 cup)**
**3 ounces Parmesan cheese, grated (about 1 cup)**

Preheat the oven to 375°F.

Using a mandoline or sharp knife, cut the zucchini lengthwise into long, thin slices. Set aside.

Pour ⅓ cup tomato sauce into an 8 × 8-inch baking dish. Add one-third of the zucchini and drizzle with some oil. Sprinkle one-third of each of the four cheeses on top. Repeat the process, creating 2 more layers, until all the ingredients are used. Bake uncovered in the oven for 40 to 45 minutes, or until bubbling on top. Allow to cool slightly before slicing.

The lasagna can be made ahead, cooled, covered, and frozen for up to 2 months. Reheat in a 300°F oven until bubbling and hot.

# pizza margherita

Have fun making these with your friends or with your kids. Add any toppings
you can think of.

**Basic Pizza Crust (recipe follows)**
**½ cup Classic Tomato Sauce (page 74)**
**¼ cup grated Asiago cheese**
**⅛ cup grated Parmesan cheese**
**6 Yogurt-Cheese Bocconcini (page 28) or provolone cheese, shredded**
**5 fresh basil leaves, cut into thin ribbons**
**1 tablespoon extra-virgin olive oil**

Preheat the oven to 300°F.

Cover the pizza with the tomato sauce. Sprinkle the Asiago and Parmesan over the
sauce and top with the Bocconcini. Sprinkle with the basil and drizzle with the oil. Bake
for 20 minutes, until the cheese bubbles. Slice into wedges and serve.

## BASIC PIZZA CRUST

MAKES ONE 6-INCH CRUST

**1 large egg**
**1 teaspoon olive oil**
**1 cup almond flour**
**¼ teaspoon kosher salt**

In a medium bowl, mix the eggs, oil, flour, and salt with a wooden spoon until well blended
and the mixture forms a ball.

Line a baking sheet with parchment paper or lightly oil a pizza pan. Using your hands,
press the dough into a 6-inch round.

Put the pizza in a cold oven and heat to 300°F. Cook until the pizza is golden brown and
crispy, about 30 minutes. The crust is now ready to be topped and returned to the oven.

# falafel with navy beans

SERVES 4 TO 6

This delicious take on the Middle Eastern standard substitutes navy beans for the usual chickpeas. It goes well with Yogurt Curry Dip (page 83) mixed with a little thinly sliced fresh mint.

2 cups dried white navy beans

1 cup almond flour, or more, if necessary

2 cloves garlic, peeled

1 tablespoon raw, unsalted tahini

1 tablespoon kosher salt

½ teaspoon baking soda

1 teaspoon cayenne pepper

½ teaspoon turmeric

½ teaspoon ground cumin

½ teaspoon ground coriander

½ cup fresh cilantro, plus extra sprigs for garnish

3 large eggs

½ cup raw, unsalted sesame seeds (if tolerated)

Vegetable oil for frying

2 lemons, cut into wedges

Rinse and pick over the beans to remove any small pebbles, and then soak in water for 24 hours, changing the water halfway through. Rinse and drain.

In a food processor, combine the beans, almond flour, garlic, tahini, salt, baking soda, cayenne, turmeric, cumin, coriander, cilantro, and eggs. Pulse until just combined. Cover and refrigerate for at least 1 hour or up to 2.

Remove the bean mixture from the refrigerator and add more almond flour if it is too sticky to handle. Pour the sesame seeds onto a plate. Form golf-ball-size patties with your hands, flatten them slightly, and roll in the seeds.

Heat 1 inch of oil in a deep skillet over medium-high heat until very hot. Fry the falafel in batches for about 3 minutes per side, until golden brown. Drain on paper towels. Add more oil to the pan and let it get hot before frying more falafel.

Serve hot, garnished with lemon wedges and cilantro sprigs.

# desserts and confections

Orange and Almond Flour Cookies

Coconut Cake

Lemon-Coconut Macaroons

Macadamia Medjool Date Cake

Tarte Tatin

Persimmon Cream Cups

Macadamia Nut Brittle

Peanut Butter Toffees

Whipped Cashew Cream

Strawberry Ice Cream

Herb Candies

**just because you are following** a healthier eating plan that doesn't allow refined sugars and starches doesn't mean you have to skip dessert or eat only fruit. The following cookies, cakes, confections, and ice cream all utilize alternative sources for sugar and starch such as honey, unsweetened coconut, and nut flours. Their wonderful taste is derived from a variety of natural flavor extracts, citrus zests, fresh fruits, and nuts.

Homemade Yogurt (page 27) plays an important role in desserts. You will find it in ice cream, cakes, and other desserts. For special occasions try making Coconut Cake (page 174). Orange and Almond Flour Cookies (page 173) make the perfect accompaniment to a cup of tea. And kids will love Strawberry Ice Cream (page 184) topped with Whipped Cashew Cream (page 183).

So go ahead and indulge with these less than sinful treats.

# orange and almond flour cookies

MAKES 60 SMALL COOKIES OR 30 LARGE ONES

These are reminiscent of French madeleine cookies, albeit crispier. I love the orange and almond flavors.

¼ cup golden brown clarified butter (see box)

8 tablespoons (1 stick) unsalted butter, softened

½ cup honey

3 cups almond flour

2 large eggs

1 tablespoon grated orange zest

2 tablespoons fresh orange juice

½ teaspoon baking soda

⅛ teaspoon kosher salt

Preheat the oven to 300°F.

Line 3 cookie sheets with parchment paper. With a pastry brush, coat the parchment with the clarified butter, reserving some for the next batch. Set aside.

In an electric mixer, beat the unsalted butter and honey until well combined. Add the almond flour and mix to incorporate. Add the eggs, 1 at a time, beating well after each addition. Add the zest, juice, baking soda, and salt, and mix well.

Spoon the batter onto the prepared cookie sheets in small circles, using about 1 table-spoon batter for each cookie. Space them about 1 inch apart. Bake for 15 to 20 minutes, or until golden. Turn off the oven and allow the cookies to sit in the oven until crispy, about 15 minutes. Remove from the oven and cool completely on the pan. Store in an airtight container for up to 4 days.

## GOLDEN BROWN CLARIFIED BUTTER

Heat the butter in a small saucepan over medium-low heat. Do not skim the top; just let the butter cook until the foam drops to the bottom and turns a deep golden color, about 2 minutes. Strain the butter through a paper-towel-lined strainer. You will have a delicious nutty clarified butter. One stick (8 tablespoons) butter will yield ⅓ cup golden brown clarified butter.

# coconut cake

While most coconut cakes are full of artificially sweetened coconut and loaded with sugar, this festive and delectable layer cake uses unsweetened coconut and honey for guilt-free indulging.

### CAKE

4 cups almond flour

1 cup honey

2 teaspoons baking soda

1 teaspoon salt

4 tablespoons unsalted butter, softened, or ¼ cup coconut oil, plus extra
  for greasing the pans

½ cup canned unsweetened coconut milk

¼ cup Homemade Yogurt (page 27)

3 large egg whites

2 teaspoons pure vanilla extract

### FROSTING

1 cup honey

¼ cup canned unsweetened coconut milk

2 tablespoons unsalted butter

1 teaspoon pure vanilla extract


3 cups grated unsweetened coconut

### TO MAKE THE CAKES

Preheat the oven to 300°F. Line the bottom of two 8-inch round cake pans with parchment paper. Use butter or coconut oil to grease the paper and the sides of the pans.

In a food processor or electric mixer, mix the almond flour, honey, baking soda, and salt until blended. Add the butter and coconut milk and mix well, stopping to scrape down the sides. Add the yogurt, egg whites, and vanilla. Mix well until very smooth, scraping down the sides frequently. Pour into the cake pans and smooth the tops.

Bake for 40 minutes, or until the cakes are golden and springy and a toothpick inserted in the center of the cake comes out clean. Remove from the oven and let sit for 10 minutes. Unmold from the pans onto a rack and let cool completely before frosting.

### TO MAKE THE FROSTING

Place the honey, coconut milk, butter, and vanilla in a food processor or electric mixer, and process until smooth.

### TO ASSEMBLE THE CAKE

Place one of the layers on a serving dish. Spread half of the frosting on the cake and sprinkle with 1 cup grated coconut. Place the second layer on top. Spread the remaining frosting on the top, allowing it to spill over the sides. Sprinkle the rest of the coconut on the top.

The cake will keep for 2 days in a plastic cake keeper or on a cake stand with a dome cover.

# lemon-coconut macaroons

MAKES ABOUT 24 COOKIES

I have always been a huge macaroon fan, but modifying the recipe for this diet made me an even bigger one! The honey is so much better tasting than the standard sugar, and the lemon zest really enhances the coconut flavor. These are chewy and delicious when cooked for 1 hour, and light and crispy when cooked longer. They are everything you would expect from a macaroon, only better.

**7 large egg whites**
**⅛ teaspoon salt**
**2½ teaspoons pure vanilla extract**
**1 tablespoon grated lemon zest**
**¾ cup honey**
**3 cups shredded unsweetened coconut**

Preheat the oven to 250° F. Line 2 cookie sheets with parchment paper.

In an electric mixer, beat the egg whites with the salt on medium-high speed until stiff peaks form. Gently fold in the vanilla, zest, honey, and coconut until thoroughly combined.

Drop tablespoonfuls of batter 1 inch apart on the cookie sheets. Bake for 1 hour and then let cool for chewy cookies. Alternatively, turn off the oven and let the cookies stay there for 3 to 4 hours, or until you are ready to serve. They will be extra crispy this way.

# macadamia medjool date cake

MAKES TWO 8½-INCH LOAVES

This is great as a dessert or a snack and can even be used as sandwich bread (with strained yogurt and sliced bananas or cucumbers). It is also delicious toasted and spread with butter, honey, and cinnamon, or Apricot Jam (page 205), or toasted and crumbled for Crunchy Homemade Cereal (page 213).

4 cups raw macadamia nuts
2 pinches of salt
20 Medjool dates, pitted
4 large eggs
½ cup Homemade Yogurt (page 27)
4 tablespoons unsalted butter, melted
2 teaspoons baking soda
2 teaspoons ground cinnamon

Preheat the oven to 300° F. Grease two 8½ × 4½-inch loaf pans.

In a food processor, puree the macadamias and salt into a paste. Transfer to a bowl. Process the dates and eggs together in the food processor until very frothy. Return the macadamias to the processor and add the yogurt, butter, baking soda, and cinnamon, and blend until smooth. Pour into the prepared loaf pans. Bake for 45 minutes to 1 hour, until a thin knife inserted in the center of the loaf comes out clean. Remove from the oven and cool completely in the pan. Unmold onto a wire rack to cool. The loaves will keep for 2 to 3 days if wrapped well in plastic or placed in an airtight container.

# tarte tatin

This is the classic French caramelized upside-down apple tart, my all-time favorite dessert, which I've adapted for the SCD. The almond flour crust goes especially well with the richly flavored apples.

### CRUST
1¼ cups almond flour, or more if needed

7 tablespoons unsalted butter, chilled and cut into pieces

⅛ teaspoon kosher salt

3 tablespoons ice water

### APPLE MIXTURE
6 tablespoons unsalted butter

8 Golden Delicious apples, peeled, quartered, and cored

½ cup honey

1 cup Homemade Crème Fraîche (page 28)

### TO MAKE THE CRUST
Place the almond flour, butter, and salt in a food processor and process for 10 seconds, or until coarse and crumblike. Add the ice water slowly and pulse about 8 times, or until the mixture just starts to come together. Do not let it form a ball. Transfer to parchment paper and flatten and form a disc shape. If the dough is too sticky, sprinkle with extra almond flour and mix in well. Wrap in parchment and freeze for at least 1 hour or up to 3 hours. Transfer to the refrigerator for 1 hour before rolling.

Preheat the oven to 375° F.

## TO PREPARE THE APPLES

Melt the butter in a deep 12-inch skillet over high heat. Stir in the apples and honey, and cook until the apples are a deep golden brown, about 18 minutes. Shake the pan occasionally to make sure the apples do not burn. Pour the apples into a 10½-inch round baking dish. Allow the apples to cool for 15 minutes.

## TO BAKE THE TART

Roll or press the crust between 2 sheets of parchment paper into a round slightly larger than the baking dish. Lay the crust on top of the apples and tuck the excess dough into the dish around the sides. Bake for 20 to 30 minutes, or until the dough is golden brown.

Remove from the oven and let sit for 5 minutes. Set a large round serving platter on top of the tart and carefully but quickly invert the tart onto the platter. Slowly lift the dish so the apples fall centered on the platter. Serve immediately or at room temperature with a dollop of crème fraîche on top of each serving. This is best made the same day it will be served.

# persimmon cream cups

SERVES 4

This is a delicious and beautiful Middle Eastern dessert. It is very important that the persimmons are at their peak of ripeness for this recipe. They should feel plump and soft to the touch.

**4 fresh, ripe Hachiya persimmons (the flesh should have the consistency of pudding)**
**¾ cup Strained Homemade Yogurt (page 28)**
**6 tablespoons honey, plus extra for serving**
**1 teaspoon pure vanilla extract**
**¼ cup unsalted raw pistachios, toasted (see page 53)**
**Fresh mint for garnish**

Cut the tops off the persimmons and set the tops aside. Scoop out the persimmon flesh, taking care not to tear the skin, and place in a medium bowl. Add the yogurt, honey, vanilla, and nuts, and mix well.

Return the mixture to the persimmon shells and cap with the persimmon tops. Chill for at least 30 minutes or up to 4 hours. Serve with a swirl of honey on the plate and some fresh mint sprigs.

# macadamia nut brittle

MAKES 2½ CUPS

Crunchy, sweet, caramelized nut brittle is often made with peanuts. You can use peanuts in this recipe if you prefer, but I just love this with macadamias. This recipe also makes a great gift for the holidays.

**3 cups chopped macadamia nuts**

**2 teaspoons salt**

**2 vanilla beans**

**2 cups honey**

**8 tablespoons (1 stick) unsalted butter, plus extra for the parchment paper**

Preheat the oven to 350° F.

Place the nuts on a cookie sheet and roast in the oven until golden brown, 12 to 14 minutes. Remove from the oven, sprinkle with salt, and set aside.

Line a cookie sheet with parchment paper, butter it, and set aside.

Split the vanilla beans lengthwise and scrape the seeds into a deep saucepan. Add the honey and simmer over low heat for 30 minutes until it reaches 275° F as measured with a candy thermometer. Stir in the nuts and butter, and cook for 1 more minute, until well mixed.

Pour the mixture on the prepared cookie sheet and place in the freezer until cool, 20 to 30 minutes.

Break into pieces and put in an airtight container. Layer the candy between wax paper or parchment, or wrap individually in plastic, wax paper, or candy wrappers. Store in the freezer for up to 2 months. The candy should be kept in the freezer until ready to be eaten, because it softens at room temperature.

# peanut butter toffees

MAKES APPROXIMATELY SIXTY-FOUR 1-INCH PIECES
This is a delicious chewy candy treat that everybody loves. Double the recipe if you like; extras (if you have any) freeze well.

2 cups honey

2 cups unsalted, crunchy, natural peanut butter

8 tablespoons (1 stick) butter, plus extra for the pan

2 tablespoons pure vanilla extract

Butter a 9 × 13-inch pan and set aside.

Heat the honey in a medium saucepan over medium-high heat until it boils. Lower the heat and simmer for 15 minutes, until the honey reaches 250° F as measured with a candy thermometer.

Stir in the peanut butter, butter, and vanilla, and cook for 1 more minute, stirring constantly. Pour the mixture into the prepared pan and freeze until cool, at least 2 or 3 hours.

Once hardened, remove from freezer and thaw until you can cut the toffee into bite-sized pieces, about 15 minutes. Wrap in candy wrappers or plastic wrap and store in the freezer for up to 2 months.

# whipped cashew cream

Use this nutty cream instead of traditional whipped cream on top of pie, alongside fruit, or on top of coffee. Also try freezing it for an interesting variation on ice cream.

1 cup raw cashews
½ cup freshly squeezed orange juice (about 2 oranges), or more if needed
2 Medjool dates, pitted
1 tablespoon honey
3 drops pure vanilla extract

Soak the nuts in 4 cups water for 3 to 4 hours, then drain.

Place the nuts in a blender with the juice, dates, honey, and vanilla. Blend on high until very smooth and frothy, stopping periodically to scrape down the sides. Add more juice if the cream is too thick.

This will keep in an airtight container for 2 days in the refrigerator. Do not freeze; this recipe needs to be made fresh each time.

# strawberry ice cream

MAKES 4 CUPS

**2 cups Homemade Yogurt of your choice (page 27)**
**1 cup fresh or frozen strawberries**
**¾ cup honey**

In a blender, puree the yogurt, strawberries, and honey until smooth. Pour into an ice cream maker and follow the manufacturer's directions for freezing. Serve immediately or store in an airtight container in the freezer for up to 2 months.

### date ice cream
Substitute 8 pitted Medjool dates for the strawberries and decrease the honey to ½ cup.

# herb candies

My daughter really wanted a candy like the ones some of the other kids had at school. Never wanting her to feel deprived, I decided to figure out a recipe using the guidelines for the diet. The results were great!

- 1 bunch fresh mint
- 1 bunch fresh lemon balm
- 1 bunch fresh marjoram
- 1 bunch fresh thyme
- 1 cup (2 sticks) unsalted butter
- 2 cups honey
- 1 teaspoon vinegar

Blend all the herbs in a blender for 3 minutes with 3 tablespoons water. Strain through a fine-mesh strainer and set aside. (Alternatively, if you have a juicer, juice all the herbs and set aside.)

Grease an 8 × 10-inch baking dish and set aside.

Melt the butter in a large saucepan set over low heat. Add the honey, vinegar, and ¼ cup water. Bring to a boil over high heat, stirring occasionally. Heat until the temperature reaches 250° F as measured on a candy thermometer, and then boil for 12 minutes, adjusting the flame to keep the temperature constant at 250° F. Add the herb juice to the honey mixture and boil until the temperature returns to 250° F. Boil for 1 minute at 250° F, then immediately pour into the prepared dish and put in the freezer until set, 3 to 4 hours.

Cut into small pieces and wrap in colorful candy wrappers or in plastic wrap and store in the freezer.

# beverages

Blood Orange–Ginger Fizz

Creamy Ginger Lemonade

Mango Lassi

Orange Delight

Sevilla Sangria

Mango Margarita

Homemade Limoncello

Coconut Milk

Moroccan Mint Tea

**many beverages are not allowed** on this diet because of the sugar they contain or problems they can cause. Some of these include juices made from concentrate, soda, beer, and rum; they are all filled with sugar. Strong coffee, decaffeinated coffee, and strong herbal teas can act as laxatives. The delicious alcoholic and nonalcoholic beverages in this chapter are all legal, however, and will not only quench your thirst but will also complement a variety of menus and add a special touch to any event you may be hosting.

Try Sevilla Sangria (page 192) for a grown-up party for twenty of your colleagues or Creamy Ginger Lemonade (page 190) for an after-school celebration for your kids and their friends. Serve Homemade Limoncello (page 194) to kick off a holiday gathering.

Try experimenting with these recipes by using different types of liquors, wines, and juices. Most of the recipes can easily be doubled or tripled to serve a crowd.

# blood orange–ginger fizz

SERVES 4

This spicy, colorful, lightly sweetened sparkling water is delicious on its own or served with a meal.

¼ **cup honey**
⅓ **cup fresh blood orange juice (about 1 orange)**
**2 tablespoons grated fresh ginger**
**One 1-liter bottle sparkling water, chilled**
**Ice cubes**

Heat the honey in a small saucepan over low heat. Add the juice and ginger, and stir well. Remove from the heat and set aside to cool. Transfer to a pitcher and chill in the refrigerator.

Add the sparkling water to the pitcher and serve over ice.

# creamy ginger lemonade

SERVES 4

This is a rich, ambrosial lemonade like you have never tasted before. Thanks to the nuts, which make it creamy, it is nourishing as well as refreshing.

**1 cup raw, unsalted almonds**
**½ cup freshly squeezed lemon juice (2 to 3 lemons)**
**3 tablespoons honey**
**One 1-inch knob ginger, peeled**
**3 cups ice cubes**
**1 lemon, cut into wedges**

In a blender, puree the almonds with 2 cups water until the nuts are very fine. Strain through a very fine sieve. Discard the nuts. Return the nutty water to the blender with the juice, honey, ginger, and ice. Blend until creamy and frothy. Pour into glasses and add a lemon slice to each glass as a garnish.

# mango lassi

SERVES 4

An Indian staple, this healthy and scrumptious smoothie-like drink is a wonderful pick-me-up in the middle of the afternoon. It can also be served as part of a nutritious breakfast.

**4 ripe mangoes, peeled, pitted, and chopped**
**2 cups Homemade Yogurt (page 27)**
**¼ cup honey (optional)**

Freeze the chopped mangoes until hard, about 2 hours. Place the mangoes, yogurt, and honey in a blender or food processor and process until smooth. Serve cold.

# orange delight

Better than the ones you had as a kid, this creamy, sweet, citrusy drink is also good for you.

2 cups freshly squeezed orange juice (4 to 5 oranges)
1 cup Homemade Yogurt (page 27)
¼ cup honey
2 cups ice cubes
1 tablespoon pure vanilla extract
1 orange, cut into wedges for garnish

Combine the juice, yogurt, honey, ice, and vanilla in a blender and process until the ice cubes are slushy. Pour into glasses and garnish with a wedge of orange.

# sevilla sangria

SERVES 6 TO 8

A wonderful chef named Stephanie Valentine (from RAW, Charlie Trotter's restaurant with Roxanne Klein) made this for a Fiesta party at my house one day. It was so delicious! This sangria uses white wine rather than the traditional red. You can use almost any fruit, so experiment with some of your favorites.

Three 750-ml bottles dry white wine
3 oranges, sliced ¼ inch thick
1 lemon, sliced ¼ inch thick
3 limes, sliced
3 fresh peaches, sliced
2 green apples, cored and sliced
1 pint fresh raspberries
1 pint fresh or frozen cherries
One 1-liter bottle sparkling water, chilled
Ice cubes

In a tall pitcher or punch bowl, combine the wine, oranges, lemon, limes, peaches, apples, raspberries, and cherries. Chill in the refrigerator for at least 2 hours or up to 5 hours. Stir in the sparkling water and serve over ice.

# mango margarita

This margarita incorporates mango and mint to create a new twist on an old classic. Honey replaces the sugar you normally find in this type of flavored margarita.

2 large fresh mangoes, peeled, pitted, and chopped (2 to 3 mangoes)
1 cup honey
3 cups ice
1 cup fresh lime juice (about 6 limes)
6 ounces tequila
1 cup chopped fresh mint leaves, plus 4 sprigs for garnish
1 cup salt
1 lime, cut into wedges
Ice cubes

In a blender, puree the mangoes and honey until smooth. Add 3 cups of the ice, juice, and tequila, and blend until slushy.

   With a mortar and pestle or in a food processor, crush the mint with the salt. Place on a plate. Rub the rim of a margarita glass with a lime wedge and then invert the glass into the mint salt to coat the edge. Fill the glass with ice cubes and pour in the mango margarita. Top with a lime wedge and a mint sprig.

# homemade limoncello

MAKES 1 (750 ML) BOTTLE

This traditional Italian aperitif is simple to make and packs a real punch. Note that this recipe needs to be made four days in advance, but the wait is worth it: Legal limoncello without the sugar!

**12 Meyer lemons, washed and dried**
**One 750-ml bottle vodka**
**2 cups honey**
**Ice cubes**

Peel the lemons in long strips with a vegetable peeler, taking care not to include the white pith. Save the lemons for another use. Place the lemon peels in a tall pitcher and pour the vodka over them. Cover and steep for 4 days at room temperature.

Stir the honey in 3 cups water in a saucepan over medium heat until well incorporated, about 3 minutes. Set aside to cool.

Pour the honey mixture over the vodka and lemon peels. Cover and let steep overnight at room temperature. Strain the limoncello into bottles and seal. Refrigerate for up to 1 month. Serve cold over ice.

# coconut milk

MAKES 1 CUP

Most canned coconut milk has added gums and/or sugars, which are not allowed on the diet. You can make coconut milk at home, however, and it will be much more flavorful than anything you can find at the store. Add it to savory or sweet dishes such as soups, stews, smoothies, and cakes, or enjoy it on its own. Choose a heavy, hairy, brown coconut without cuts, bruises, or cracks. Make sure that you hear liquid sloshing around inside when you shake the coconut.

**1 medium coconut**

Preheat the oven to 350° F.

Pierce the spots that look like eyes with a corkscrew, drain the liquid from inside, and set aside.

Place the coconut on a rimmed baking sheet and bake for 20 minutes, until the shell begins to crack. Remove from the oven and let cool.

Use a hammer to break the shell in several places. Carefully cut away the flesh and then peel off the tough brown skin from the white flesh with a vegetable peeler or a knife. Chop or grate the flesh in a food processor.

Bring 2 cups water to a boil. Pour it over the coconut in the food processor and blend until very smooth. Strain through a very fine sieve lined with cheesecloth. Press against the coconut to squeeze out all the liquid, then discard the coconut. The coconut milk can be used immediately or cooled and refrigerated for up to 3 days or frozen for up to 2 months.

**quick coconut milk**

To make 1 cup, bring 1 cup water to a boil. Combine the boiling water and 1 cup unsweetened coconut flakes in a blender or food processor and process until very fine. Strain through cheesecloth or a fine sieve, pressing to extract all the liquid.

# moroccan mint tea

MAKES 6 CUPS

Whenever my children get run-down or get stomachaches, I give them this fragrant medicinal tea, because mint is very soothing for the stomach. This tea is very good served chilled as well.

**1 big bunch fresh mint**
**3 tablespoons honey**

Place the mint in a large teapot. Bring 6 cups water to a rolling boil and pour over the mint to fill the pot. Steep for 3 minutes, then add the honey to the pot, stir well, and serve.

# breakfast

Eggs Florentine Benedict

Shirred Eggs with Chive Yogurt

Truffled Scrambled Eggs

Brie, Chive, and Shiitake Omelet

Breakfast Pork Sausages

Currant Scones with Apricot Butter

Banana Macadamia Bread

Blueberry Almond Muffins

Pecan Waffles with Sautéed Bananas and Cinnamon Honey

French Toast with Orange Honey Butter

Cinnamon Pancakes

Banana Coconut Fritters with Honey

Crunchy Homemade Cereal

**for those following the scd,** traditional breakfast foods such as breads, muffins, scones, cereals, waffles, and pancakes are not an option because they all contain sugar and starch. The good news, however, is that breakfast on this diet is still delicious. There are so many possibilities that you will never miss your starch-filled breakfasts again!

Eggs play a key part in this diet and in breakfast in particular. Elaine Gottschall considered them a truly perfect food: high in protein, low in fat, and completely legal. They play a starring role in most of the breakfast foods offered here and are an important ingredient in pancakes and baked goods.

The dishes in this chapter range in their versatility. Some can be served at a chic brunch-time affair, such as Brie, Chive, and Shiitake Omelet (page 202) and French Toast with Orange Honey Butter (page 210), while others are better for kids on the go, such as Blueberry Almond Muffins (page 207) and Crunchy Homemade Cereal (page 213). By doubling batches and freezing half the recipe, you'll have healthy and satisfying dishes at the ready for quick weekday breakfasts or a leisurely Sunday brunch.

# eggs florentine benedict

SERVES 4

I like the sautéed spinach of Eggs Florentine but can't forgo the smoky, salty bacon and rich hollandaise sauce of traditional eggs Benedict—so I combined the two in what has become my family's new brunch favorite. The spinach replaces the usual English muffin as a bed for the poached eggs, and I prefer thinly sliced prosciutto to thick Canadian bacon, which is frequently made with sugars and additives.

**Sautéed Spinach (recipe follows)**
**4 thin slices prosciutto**
**4 large eggs, poached (see box, page 47)**
**Hollandaise Sauce (page 77)**
**Salt and freshly ground pepper to taste**

Divide the spinach among 4 plates. Lay a slice of prosciutto on top of each and then top with an egg. Pour the hollandaise over the top and season with salt and pepper.

## SAUTÉED SPINACH

SERVES 4

**1 tablespoon olive oil**
**1 tablespoon unsalted butter**
**2 tablespoons minced shallots**
**8 ounces fresh spinach**
**Salt and freshly ground pepper to taste**

Heat the oil and butter in a large skillet over medium heat and add the shallots. Sauté for 1 minute, add the spinach, and stir. Add the salt and pepper, and cook for 2 to 3 more minutes, until the spinach has wilted. Serve hot.

# shirred eggs with chive yogurt

SERVES 4

On special occasions my mother used to make this old-fashioned recipe for eggs baked with heavy cream in individual ramekins. I actually prefer this SCD modified version that uses Homemade Yogurt (page 27) in place of the cream and remains the ultimate comfort food for me.

¼ cup Homemade Yogurt (page 27)
1 tablespoon snipped fresh chives
4 teaspoons unsalted butter
8 large eggs
Salt and freshly ground pepper to taste

Preheat the oven to 400°F.

Mix the yogurt and chives together in a bowl and set aside.

Using 4- to 6-ounce gratin dishes or ramekins (they should be large enough to hold no more than 2 eggs each), melt 1 teaspoon butter in each dish in the oven. When the butter has melted, swirl it around each dish to coat the bottom. Crack 2 eggs in each dish, season with salt and pepper, and top each one with 1 tablespoon chive yogurt. Cover with a piece of parchment paper and bake for 10 to 15 minutes, until the eggs are set. Uncover and serve hot.

# truffled scrambled eggs

SERVES 4

This is a simple yet utterly indulgent brunch dish: rich and creamy scrambled eggs showered with shaved truffles. Fresh white truffles are heavenly in season, which is usually November through January, but you can also use black ones (fresh or canned), truffle oil, truffle butter, or even a pinch of truffle salt. All of these are easier to find and will elevate these homey eggs to something spectacular without breaking the bank.

**10 large eggs and 4 large egg yolks**
**Salt and freshly ground pepper to taste**
**1 tablespoon unsalted butter**
**1 teaspoon olive oil**
**1 tablespoon white truffle oil or 1 small fresh white truffle (about
    $\frac{1}{2}$ ounce)**

In a medium bowl, beat the eggs with the yolks and season with salt and pepper.

Heat the butter and oil in a large sauté pan over medium heat and swirl to coat the pan. Add the eggs and cook until the eggs just start to set on the bottom, 1 or 2 minutes. Adjust the heat to low and begin to break up or "scramble" the eggs with a wooden spoon. Cook the eggs slowly, scraping the bottom of the pan and pulling up the curds until the eggs are fully cooked to your liking. This could take up to 10 minutes.

If using truffle oil, stir it into the eggs. Divide the eggs among 4 warm plates. If using fresh truffle, shave it over the top. Serve immediately.

# brie, chive, and shiitake omelet

SERVES 2

This flavorful omelet combines the earthiness of mushrooms with the smooth creaminess of Brie, resulting in a hearty yet sophisticated breakfast dish that would also not be out of place at lunch or dinner.

**2 tablespoons unsalted butter**

**2 teaspoons olive oil**

**2 ounces (½ cup) fresh shiitake mushrooms, stemmed and caps roughly chopped**

**Salt and freshly ground pepper to taste**

**4 large eggs**

**1 tablespoon snipped fresh chives**

**2 ounces (about ¼ cup) Brie cheese, rind removed**

Preheat the broiler.

Heat 1 tablespoon butter and 1 teaspoon oil in a large sauté pan over medium heat. Add the mushrooms, salt, and pepper, and stir. Cook for 5 minutes, until golden brown.

Beat the eggs, season with salt and pepper, and whisk in the chives.

Add the remaining tablespoon of butter and the remaining teaspoon of oil to the pan. Stir the mushrooms to distribute them evenly. Pour the eggs over the mushrooms, tilting the pan to coat them evenly. Cook for 2 minutes.

Place the cheese evenly on top of the eggs. Place under the broiler for 1 or 2 minutes, until the cheese melts and the egg is cooked on top. Remove from the oven and use a spatula to roll up the omelet from end to end. Cut in half and divide between 2 warm plates. Serve immediately.

# breakfast pork sausages

If possible, use organic pork for these delicious sausages. It is important to cook them over low heat, because otherwise the honey and apple juice may burn.

**2 pounds ground pork**
**3 Medjool dates, pitted and finely minced**
**2 tablespoons honey**
**2 tablespoons apple juice**
**2 teaspoons finely chopped fresh thyme**
**2 teaspoons finely chopped fresh sage**
**2 teaspoons finely chopped marjoram**
**½ teaspoon freshly grated nutmeg**
**Pinch of cayenne pepper**
**Salt and freshly ground pepper to taste**
**3 tablespoons olive oil**

In a large bowl, mix together the ground pork, dates, honey, apple juice, thyme, sage, marjoram, nutmeg, cayenne, salt, and pepper by hand. Form into 3-inch patties about ½ inch thick. (These can be made in advance and refrigerated for 3 days.)

Heat the oil in a large skillet over low heat. Add the patties and cook until browned on both sides and cooked through, about 20 minutes. Serve hot.

# currant scones with apricot butter

MAKES 2 DOZEN 3-INCH SCONES

These scones, made primarily from almond flour and yogurt, are a more healthful variation than the standard white flour and butter scone. Try the apricot butter accompaniment with toasted Cashew Bread (page 160), too.

¼ cup Apricot Jam (recipe follows)
8 tablespoons (1 stick) unsalted butter, softened
3 cups almond flour
1 teaspoon baking soda
2 tablespoons honey
½ cup Homemade Yogurt (page 27)
1 cup currants
1 large egg yolk

To make the apricot butter, mix together the jam and butter and set aside. (Can be made 4 days in advance and kept in the refrigerator.) Preheat the oven to 325° F. Line a baking sheet with parchment paper.

In a food processor, mix the almond flour, baking soda, honey, and yogurt until well blended. Transfer to a bowl and stir in the currants. Drop in heaping tablespoonfuls onto the prepared baking sheet, leaving an inch between each spoonful. Beat the egg yolk with 1 tablespoon water to make an egg wash. Brush the scones with the egg wash. Bake for 20 minutes or until golden.

Serve hot or at room temperature with apricot butter.

# APRICOT JAM

**2 tablespoons freshly squeezed lemon juice**
**½ to 1 cup honey, to taste**
**3 to 3½ pounds fresh apricots (15 to 20), halved and pitted**

In a medium saucepan over low heat, combine the lemon juice and ½ cup honey. Stir well and simmer until the mixture is thick, about 10 minutes. Add the apricots and mix well. Raise the heat to medium and mash the apricots with a potato masher or a fork. Boil for 3 minutes. Stir in the remaining honey to taste if needed and lower the heat. Simmer for 30 minutes or so, until thickened. Remove from the heat and set aside to cool completely. Place in airtight containers and refrigerate for up to 2 weeks.

# banana macadamia bread

MAKES TWO 8½-INCH LOAVES

This rich and satisfying bread is great for breakfast, dessert, or a snack. You can also make muffins out of this recipe if you prefer (bake for about 30 minutes or until golden brown). Top with Homemade Crème Fraîche (page 28) or Apricot Jam (page 205).

**16 ounces (4 cups) raw, unsalted macadamia nuts**
**¾ cup honey**
**4 large eggs**
**4 very ripe bananas, mashed**
**4 tablespoons butter, melted**
**1 teaspoon pure vanilla extract**
**1 teaspoon baking soda**

Preheat the oven to 300° F. Grease two 1.5-quart (8½ × 4½ × 2½) loaf pans and line the bottoms with parchment paper.

Place all the ingredients in a food processor and process until smooth. Pour the batter into the prepared loaf pans and bake for 55 to 60 minutes.

Turn off the oven and leave the loaves in until the oven has cooled. Remove from the pans and serve immediately or wrap in plastic wrap and store in the refrigerator for up to 4 days.

# blueberry almond muffins

These muffins taste best served right out of the oven with butter and honey on top. They also make a good lunch box snack the next day. Try substituting chopped ripe bananas or peaches or other fruit for the blueberries. Change the almond flour to pecan or cashew flour for a different taste. Chopped nuts, raisins, or coconut can be added as well. The variations are endless.

3 cups almond flour
2 large eggs
8 tablespoons (1 stick) unsalted butter, melted
¼ cup honey
1 teaspoon baking soda
2 teaspoons pure vanilla extract
Pinch of salt
1½ cups fresh or frozen blueberries

Preheat the oven to 300° F. Line a standard 12-cup muffin pan with paper cupcake liners.

In a food processor, puree the almond flour, eggs, butter, honey, baking soda, vanilla, and salt until smooth. Transfer to a bowl and gently fold in the blueberries. With a big spoon, scoop the batter into the prepared muffin pan. Bake for about 40 minutes, or until golden brown. Serve warm or at room temperature.

# pecan waffles with sautéed bananas and cinnamon honey

SERVES 8 TO 10

Keep in mind that these waffles will cook a little bit faster than a flour waffle because of the honey in the batter. If you don't have a waffle iron, try using the batter for pancakes. Top with toasted chopped pecans, if desired.

WAFFLES

2 cups unsalted raw pecans

4 large eggs

8 tablespoons (1 stick) unsalted butter, melted, plus more for greasing
  the waffle iron

¼ cup honey

1½ teaspoons pure vanilla extract

½ teaspoon baking soda

Pinch of salt

SAUTÉED BANANAS

1 tablespoon unsalted butter

1 teaspoon coconut oil or vegetable oil

3 very ripe bananas, sliced

1 cup honey

1 tablespoon ground cinnamon

TO MAKE THE WAFFLES

Preheat a waffle iron according to the manufacturer's directions. Preheat the oven to 200° F.

In a food processor, pulverize the pecans until finely ground. Add the eggs, butter, honey, vanilla, baking soda, and salt, and blend well.

Grease the waffle iron using a partially wrapped stick of cold butter. Hold the butter by its wrapped end and rub the other end all over the waffle iron's cooking surface. Add ¼ cup batter and cook for a few minutes, until golden brown. Set right on the oven rack to crisp up and keep warm while you cook more.

### TO PREPARE THE BANANAS

Melt the butter with the oil in a sauté pan over medium heat. Add the bananas and cook for about 6 minutes, turning once, until golden brown. Set aside.

### TO SERVE

Mix the honey and cinnamon until well blended.

Place the waffles on warmed plates and top with the bananas, honey, and cinnamon, and serve.

# french toast with orange honey butter

Made from homemade nut "bread," this French toast is rich in flavor and delicate in texture due to the whole-egg batter.

2 large eggs
1 teaspoon ground cinnamon
1 teaspoon pure vanilla extract
Pinch of salt
Four ½-inch slices Cashew Bread (page 160)
1 tablespoon salted butter
1 teaspoon coconut oil or vegetable oil
¼ cup Orange Honey Butter (recipe follows)

In a shallow dish, whisk together the eggs, cinnamon, vanilla, and salt. Add the bread slices and soak for 10 minutes. Flip them over and soak for 10 more minutes.

Heat a skillet over medium-high heat and add the butter and oil. Place the bread in the skillet and sauté for about 2 minutes on each side, or until golden brown.

Top each piece of toast with Orange Honey Butter and serve hot.


## ORANGE HONEY BUTTER

MAKES ABOUT ¾ CUP

8 tablespoons (1 stick) unsalted butter, softened
5 tablespoons honey
1 teaspoon grated orange zest
2 tablespoons freshly squeezed orange juice

In an electric mixer, beat the butter, honey, orange zest, and juice until fluffy, 3 to 4 minutes. Use immediately, store tightly wrapped in the refrigerator for up to 1 week, or freeze for up to 3 weeks. Return to room temperature before using.

# cinnamon pancakes

MAKES 1 DOZEN SILVER-DOLLAR-SIZE PANCAKES

Imagine pancakes that are actually good for you and taste better than the white flour kind! A great protein-packed start to your day, these will give you energy all morning. Drizzle them with melted butter and honey before serving.

1 cup whole organic cashews

3 large eggs

2 tablespoons Homemade Yogurt (page 27)

½ teaspoon baking soda

1 tablespoon honey

1 teaspoon ground cinnamon

¼ teaspoon pure vanilla extract

Pinch of salt

1 tablespoon coconut oil or vegetable oil

Grind the cashews into a paste in a food processor. Add the eggs, yogurt, baking soda, honey, cinnamon, vanilla, and salt, and blend well.

Heat the coconut oil in a large frying pan over medium-low heat. Pour the batter into small pools and cook for 2 to 3 minutes, until golden. Flip and cook for an additional 1 or 2 minutes.

Serve hot.

# banana coconut fritters with honey

MAKES ABOUT 18

These fritters are easy, fast, and good because they aren't deep-fried. They are also very nutritious and satisfying. My kids eat piles of them.

**4 large eggs**
**2 very ripe bananas**
**½ cup unsweetened shredded dried coconut**
**About 4 tablespoons unsalted butter**
**About 4 teaspoons coconut oil or vegetable oil**
**Honey to taste**

Beat the eggs in a medium bowl. Add the bananas and coconut, and mash with a fork.

Heat 1 tablespoon butter and 1 teaspoon oil in a large sauté pan over medium heat. Using a small ladle or large spoon, drop in 2 tablespoons of the banana mixture per fritter. Cook in batches for about 1 or 2 minutes per side until golden brown. Set aside on a warmed plate. Repeat with the remaining batter, butter, and oil.

Drizzle with honey and serve hot.

# crunchy homemade cereal

SERVES 4

This satisfying and delicious homemade granola-type cereal contains more nutrients than most store-bought varieties, and much less sugar. It uses left-over Blueberry Almond Muffins (page 207) as the base and has nuts, coconut, and diced fruit for sweetness and crunch.

**4 Blueberry Almond Muffins (page 207)**
**½ cup raw unsalted walnuts, lightly toasted (see page 53)**
**½ cup shredded unsweetened coconut, toasted (page 53)**
**½ cup home-dehydrated banana chips, raspberry slices, or favorite fruit**
**¼ cup raisins**
**2 cups Homemade Yogurt (page 27)**
**¼ cup honey (optional)**

Preheat the oven to 200°F.

Crumble the muffins onto a parchment-lined cookie sheet. Toast in the oven for about 30 minutes, until crunchy. Allow to cool completely.

Mix the muffins with the nuts, coconut, dried fruit, and raisins. Set aside.

Place ½ cup yogurt in each of 4 serving bowls. Top with the muffin mixture, drizzle the top with honey, if desired, and serve.

# just for kids

Cucumber and Celery Boats with Herbed Farmer Cheese

Cheese Soufflé

Beef Jerky

Herb and Garlic Turkey Skewers

Honey-Garlic Chicken Drummettes

Peach Pocket Pies

Banana Boats

Honey-Coconut Doughnuts

Frozen Banana Sticks with Peanut Butter

Smoothie Popsicles

Honey Lollipops

**as any parent knows,** getting kids to eat food that is good for them can be a challenge, and even more so with kids who are sick. And because they are sick, you don't want them to feel different or deprived.

While kids can enjoy virtually all the recipes in this book, this chapter contains dishes especially dedicated to their likes and dislikes. In fact, my daughter's friends love coming to our house to eat! Who can resist Frozen Banana Sticks with Peanut Butter (page 226), perfect for a snack or dessert? It's hard to say no to Honey-Coconut Doughnuts (page 225), a sweet treat that's actually good for you. And Honey-Garlic Chicken Drummettes (page 221) are the perfect food for kids' parties.

One great way to get your children to eat a meal with a variety of fruits, vegetables, and protein is simply to arrange little groups of each on a large platter and watch the kids dig in. Try fruits such as apples, raspberries, strawberries, and raisins; vegetables such as carrots, celery sticks with peanut butter (no additives), English peas, and sliced cucumbers; and protein such as hard-boiled eggs, cheeses cut into strips or cubes, peanuts (in the shell), raw and unsalted walnuts or almonds or pecans.

A perfect high-energy, nutrient-rich lunch box snack is dried fruit chips. Use a food dehydrator to dehydrate just about any fruit. Try slices of banana, strawberry, mango, pineapple, peaches, coconut shavings, apples, and pears. The longer you dehydrate, the crisper they will be. You can also dehydrate strawberry slices or banana slices in half the time and have a substitute chewing gum (chewing gum is illegal on SCD).

Parents can feel good about serving these healthful and flavorful snacks that their kids will really want to eat.

# cucumber and celery boats with herbed farmer cheese

SERVES 3 TO 6

These crunchy, creamy snacks are yummy and fun for kids to eat and are nutritious as well.

**3 medium cucumbers, peeled, halved lengthwise, and seeded, or 3 large celery stalks, strings removed and halved crosswise**
**1 cup Herbed Farmer Cheese (page 45)**

Simply fill each "boat" with the cheese mixture and serve.

# cheese soufflé

SERVES 4

While the name may sound grown-up, kids love this dish. This soufflé is a lighter improvement on the classic and is much simpler to make, too. You can use any aged cheese, including cheddar, Monterey Jack, Gruyère, Gouda, Emmentaler, or Manchego (my favorite). Try adding spinach or different herbs for a variety of flavor.

**4 tablespoons unsalted butter, melted**
**½ cup plus 2 tablespoons freshly grated Parmesan cheese**
**4 large eggs, separated**
**1¼ cups Homemade Yogurt (page 27)**
**Salt and freshly ground pepper to taste**
**Pinch of freshly grated nutmeg**
**8 ounces aged cheese, grated (2 cups)**
**3 egg whites**

Pour 1 tablespoon butter into each of four 8-ounce ramekins and swirl to coat the bottom and sides. Divide 2 tablespoons Parmesan cheese among the ramekins and shake them to distribute the cheese evenly. Set in the refrigerator to chill.

Preheat the oven to 400°F.

In a large bowl, whisk together the egg yolks, yogurt, salt, pepper, and nutmeg until smooth. Stir in the aged cheese.

Using an electric mixer, beat the egg whites on medium-high speed until stiff. Fold into the cheese batter in 3 batches. Pour into the prepared ramekins and dust the tops with the remaining ½ cup of Parmesan cheese. Place on a baking sheet. Bake for 5 minutes, then lower the oven temperature to 325°F and bake for another 25 minutes, until golden and puffed.

Serve immediately.

# beef jerky

This chewy additive-free jerky is a great alternative to the artificial store-bought variety. If using a dehydrator instead of an oven, set it to 145° F and dry for 8 hours.

**1 pound top sirloin, sliced paper-thin (ask the butcher to slice it, slightly frozen, on the meat slicer)**

**¼ cup extra-virgin olive oil**

**2 cloves garlic, minced**

**Salt and freshly ground pepper to taste**

Preheat the oven to 175° F.

In a large bowl, mix together the meat, oil, garlic, salt, and pepper, coating the meat well on both sides. Lay the meat on cookie sheets and place in the oven. Leave the meat overnight, 8 to 10 hours, until dried but still a little chewy. Store in a sealed container in the refrigerator for up to 1 week.

# herb and garlic turkey skewers

SERVES 4 TO 6

Kids love turkey, and they love eating anything on a stick. Here is a flavorful and creative way for them to enjoy both.

¼ cup olive oil
1 tablespoon grated lemon zest
2 tablespoons freshly squeezed lemon juice
3 cloves garlic, minced
¼ teaspoon ground oregano
½ teaspoon dried fines herbes (optional)
Salt and freshly ground pepper to taste
1 pound skinless, boneless turkey breast, cut into 1 × 4-inch strips
10 bamboo skewers

In a bowl, stir together the oil, zest, juice, garlic, oregano, fines herbes, salt, and pepper with a fork until well mixed. Set the turkey pieces in the mixture and coat well. Cover with plastic and place in the refrigerator for at least 1 hour or overnight.

Soak the bamboo skewers in water for 30 minutes. Preheat a grill to medium.

Thread the marinated turkey onto the bamboo skewers; discard the marinade. Grill the skewers until the turkey is cooked through, 8 to 10 minutes on each side. Serve hot.

# honey-garlic chicken drummettes

MAKES 20

These sweet little succulent drummettes will disappear quickly. The flavorful bites are perfect as a snack or meal and are quite an improvement over your typical chicken nugget.

1 cup olive oil

1 teaspoon ground oregano

1 tablespoon paprika

6 cloves garlic, minced

1 small yellow onion, finely minced

2 tablespoons freshly grated orange zest (about 2 oranges)

Salt and freshly ground pepper to taste

20 chicken drummettes (about 2 pounds)

½ cup honey

2 oranges, cut into wedges, for garnish

In a bowl, stir together the oil, oregano, paprika, garlic, onion, zest, salt, and pepper with a fork until well mixed. Add the drummettes to the mixture and turn them to coat well. Cover with plastic and place in the refrigerator for at least 1 hour or up to 6.

Preheat the oven to 400°F.

Place the drummettes in a roasting pan; discard the marinade. Roast for 40 to 45 minutes, or until golden brown and cooked through. Remove from the oven, drizzle with the honey, and roast for 5 more minutes. Serve on a platter with the orange wedges.

# peach pocket pies

These individual pies are a delectable dessert for kids and adults alike, and
they are a perfect summertime treat when peaches are at their ripest.

### CRUST

3 cups almond flour

8 tablespoons (1 stick) unsalted butter, cut into small pieces and chilled

1 large egg

½ cup honey

½ teaspoon baking soda

Pinch of kosher salt

1 tablespoon grated orange zest

### FILLING

8 medium ripe yellow or white peaches, peeled and cut into small pieces

½ cup honey

¼ cup freshly squeezed lemon juice (about 1 lemon)

½ teaspoon ground cinnamon

⅛ teaspoon freshly grated nutmeg

⅛ teaspoon ground cloves

1 egg

### TO MAKE THE CRUST

In a food processor or electric mixer, blend the almond flour, butter, egg, honey, baking
soda, salt, and zest until the mixture comes together to form a ball. Flatten and wrap in
plastic wrap. Refrigerate for at least 1 hour or up to 4, or freeze for up to 2 weeks. Defrost
overnight in the refrigerator before proceeding.

### TO MAKE THE FILLING

Combine the peaches, honey, juice, cinnamon, nutmeg, and cloves in a large saucepan and bring to a boil over high heat. Lower the heat and simmer the peaches for 20 minutes, until they are very tender and the mixture has thickened. Set aside to cool. The peaches can be covered and refrigerated for up to 1 week at this point.

### TO BAKE THE PIES

Preheat the oven to 300° F.

Divide the dough into 6 pieces. On a large baking sheet covered with parchment paper, press out the dough into 6 circles using your fingers; the dough should be quite thin, about ⅛ inch thick. Spoon some of the peach filling on the center of each circle and fold one side over the other to make half moons. Pinch the edges together to seal. Beat the egg with 1 tablespoon cold water and then brush the egg wash over each peach pocket.

Bake for 40 minutes, then turn off the oven and leave the pies in it for 10 minutes, or until golden brown. Serve warm. These are best if served within 4 hours of baking.

# banana boats

We used to make a variation of these dessert packets when I was a kid, putting them on the hot coals of a grill or a beach bonfire. Although I no longer use chocolate and marshmallows, the bananas, peanut butter, and dried fruit that replaces them become gooey and fragrant when heated. You can also cook these pouches in the oven.

**4 ripe bananas, peeled and split lengthwise**
**½ cup chunky natural peanut butter**
**½ cup shredded unsweetened coconut**
**¼ cup raisins**
**¼ cup dried unsulfured apricots**
**¼ cup finely chopped raw unsalted pecans**
**½ cup honey**

Preheat the oven to 400°F or heat a grill to medium.

Cut four 10 × 12-inch sheets of aluminum foil and line them with an 8 × 10-inch square of parchment paper.

Put 1 banana on each sheet of parchment-lined foil.

Spread with one-fourth of the peanut butter and sprinkle with one-fourth of the coconut, raisins, apricots, and pecans. Drizzle the honey all over the top. Fold up all 4 sides to form a pouch, leaving a small opening on top.

Place the pouches on a baking sheet and bake for 15 to 20 minutes, until the bananas are warm and the peanut butter has melted. Alternatively, place the pouches directly on hot coals and cook for 20 minutes. Unwrap and dig in.

# honey-coconut doughnuts

MAKES 1 DOZEN

These baked doughnuts cut out sugar and white flour but not taste. Serve them hot, right out of the oven. You will need a doughnut-shaped mold with a 3-inch diameter.

½ cup clarified butter (see page 77)

2¼ cups almond flour

2 tablespoons unsalted butter, softened

2½ teaspoons baking soda

1½ cups honey

1 cup Homemade Yogurt (page 27)

2 teaspoons pure vanilla extract

2 large egg yolks

4 large egg whites

¼ teaspoon kosher salt

1 cup shredded unsweetened coconut, toasted (see page 53)

Preheat the oven to 300°F.

Grease the doughnut pans with the clarified butter.

Combine the almond flour, unsalted butter, and baking soda in a large bowl and mix well. Add ½ cup honey, yogurt, vanilla, and egg yolks, and beat with a wooden spoon until well blended. Set aside.

In an electric mixer, beat the egg whites with the salt on medium-high speed until stiff peaks form, 5 to 7 minutes. Gently fold the egg whites into the almond flour mixture.

Spoon the batter into the doughnut molds, filling them not quite to the top. Bake for 25 minutes, or until golden. Remove from the oven and set aside to cool.

Heat the remaining 1 cup honey until just warm. Dip the tops of each doughnut in the honey and sprinkle with the toasted coconut. Serve warm or at room temperature. These will keep for 2 to 3 days in an airtight container.

## frozen banana sticks with peanut butter

SERVES 4

These quick, easy treats are a hit with kids. Serve them as an after-school treat or for dessert.

4 ripe (with spots) bananas, peeled
4 Popsicle sticks
¼ cup chunky natural peanut butter
¼ cup shredded dried unsweetened coconut

Skewer the bananas at one end to about the middle of each banana with a Popsicle stick. Spread the peanut butter all over the bananas and sprinkle with coconut. Cover each banana with plastic wrap or lay on a plate or glass dish. Freeze for at least 2 hours, until hard, or for up to 2 weeks.

## smoothie popsicles

MAKES ABOUT 12

2 cups freshly squeezed orange juice
1 cup Homemade Yogurt (page 27)
1 ripe banana, peeled
8 strawberries, hulled

Puree the juice, yogurt, banana, and strawberries in a blender. Pour into ice pop molds and cover with the tops. Freeze for at least 3 hours, until frozen, or up to 1 week.

Unmold by dipping the outside of the mold in lukewarm water for 10 seconds.

# honey lollipops

MAKES 36

These are a sweet and satisfying candy treat without sugar. You'll need lollipop sticks and 2 lollipop molds, which can be found at most craft stores. You'll also need a candy thermometer.

**Vegetable oil**
**36 lollipop sticks**
**2 cups honey**
**1 teaspoon apple cider vinegar**
**1 teaspoon pure mint, orange, or lemon extract**

Coat the lollipop molds with vegetable oil, put the sticks in place, and set aside.

In a heavy-bottomed saucepan over medium-low heat, heat the honey, ½ cup water, and vinegar until boiling. Stir and then lower the heat slightly until the mixture simmers aggressively. Cook for about 15 minutes, or until the temperature reaches 300° F as measured on a candy thermometer. Remove from the heat and carefully stir in the extract.

Working quickly, place 1 teaspoonful of the mixture in each mold. (You might have to reheat the mixture over low heat if it starts to thicken.) Set aside to cool.

Remove the lollipops from the molds according to the instructions that come with the molds, because they vary. Wrap individually either in candy wrappers or plastic wrap. Store in an airtight container in the freezer until they are ready to be eaten or up to 2 months.

# resources

Here are Web sites that I have found useful in following the SCD. You can find support groups online by going to these Web sites and also writing to the Long Island List-Serv (SCD-list-subscribe@longisland.com) and signing up for their helpful forum.

### www.breakingtheviciouscycle.info
This was created and monitored by SCD founder Elaine Gottschall, and now her daughter Judy Herod oversees it. You can check their links section for more sites and updated information. It also has links for other countries.

### www.scdrecipe.com
Run by cookbook author Raman Prasad, this Web site has some great SCD recipes. Prasad is the author of *Adventures in the Family Kitchen* and *Colitis and Me: A Story of Recovery*.

### www.scdiet.org
Provides links to success stories, support groups, medical professionals sympathetic to the SCD, recipes, and more.

### www.healingcrow.com
A grassroots charity with a mission to inform the public about viable nondrug-related approaches for treating chronic illnesses.

**www.pecanbread.com**

This site, geared to parents of kids using SCD, has a special emphasis on autism. It also has some good recipes.

**www.lucyskitchenshop.com**

This online retailer offers many helpful foods and equipment for following the SCD, such as almond flour, yogurt starter, and acidophilus capsules.

# acknowledgments

Many people helped make this book possible. First and foremost, I would like to thank Elaine Gottschall for her overwhelming generosity of time. In developing the Specific Carbohydrate Diet, she helped so many people live free from pain and medication, allowing them to lead normal lives. She devoted her life to assisting others. She sent me at least a hundred personal e-mails, answering all my questions, and I am not the only one! Her indefatigable campaign to reach out to as many people as she could still amazes me and has been a powerful inspiration to me. She left a huge legacy and a wealth of information that has and will continue to aid others.

My thanks also to Judy (Elaine's daughter) and Stuart Herod for their encouragment and support.

My thanks also go to: Rori Trovato, a hugely talented food stylist and incredible cook who helped me with this project from the very beginning to the very end. Rori showed me the ropes and supported me. I don't think I could have done this without her, a true friend.

Coleen O'Shea, my excellent agent, who believed in this project from its inception and helped me continuously, overseeing each and every aspect to its conclusion.

Dr. Cara Familian Natterson, our inspired pediatrician, who followed my daughter's course through sickness into wellness and recommends Elaine's book to her patients because she grasps the importance of this diet.

Dr. Dale Figtree, our wonderful nutritionist, who first introduced me to Elaine's diet and helped my child get well.

Luca Trovato for his wonderful photography, thoughtful vision, and careful eye.

Lucy Rosset, Elaine's dear and caring friend, whose Web site (www.lucyskitchenshop.com) provides me with ingredients for the diet and who at the beginning spent endless hours on the phone teaching and helping me.

Tracey Still and Carrie Tinkham, for testing and retesting a whole new way of cooking!

Pamela Cannon, for her wonderful editing skills and attention to detail!

Rica Allannic, my fantastic, meticulous editor (nothing gets by her) at Clarkson Potter, who inspired me with great ideas and helpful advice.

Pam Krauss, executive editor at Clarkson Potter, for giving the green light to this book and guiding it in the right direction.

Ina Garten, the little birdie who brought my idea to my publisher, whom I have yet to meet and thank in person!

Special thanks go to Barbara Alpert, Michael Flutie, Brian Hodges, Jennifer Smith Hale, Gina Tolleson, Liseanne Frankfurt, Priscilla Woolworth, Lisa Bittan, Carol Wolper, Stephanie Valentine, Sandy Hill, Nancy Simon, Patsy Hirsch, Susan Ciminelli, Holly Palance, and Maggie Ward.

I am also grateful to: my parents: my lovely mother, Mary Conrad, for her recipes and for teaching me about cooking in the first place; and my amazing father, Barnaby Conrad, for being a wonderful pal and teaching me everything I know and then some.

My brother, Barnaby Conrad III, for his constant guidance and wisdom.

My sweet and talented sister, Cayetana Conrad, for her sensitivity.

My family for supporting me through this and for eating all of my trial-and-errors. My incredible children, Luisa and Fernanda, who inspire and amaze me every day. My wonderful husband, David, my best friend and great love, who has always been there for me and made it possible for me to take the time to write this book.

# index

Stew, Moroccan, with
Cashews, Saffron, and
Currants, 110–11
Stock, Basic, 55
Stock, Basic, Infused, 63
stock, buying, 23
Thighs, Asian Skewered
Peanut, with Asparagus,
115
Tom Yum Kai with Coconut Milk
and Lemongrass Infusion,
62
chile(s):
Curry Paste, 112–13
Dipping Sauce, Spicy, 34
Ground Beef Chili with Navy
Beans, 120–21
Hot and Sour Soup, 66
Infused Basic Chicken Stock,
63
Chili, Ground Beef, with Navy
Beans, 120–21
Chips and crackers:
Butternut Squash Chips, 164
Buttery Herb and Garlic
Crackers, 159
Cashew Butter Tortillas, 157
Havarti Dill Quesadillas, 158
Lime and Sea Salt Tortilla
Chips, 156
Middle Eastern Pita Chips, 156
Parmesan Crackers, 61
Chutney, Mango-Currant, 37
Chutney, Tomato, 139
Cinnamon Pancakes, 211
clams:
Shellfish Paella with Zucchini
Rice and Homemade
Chorizo, 104–5
Steamed, in White Wine,
Thyme, and Butter, 103
coconut:
Banana Boats, 224
Banana Fritters with Honey,
212
Cake, 174–75
Crunchy Homemade Cereal,
213
Frozen Banana Sticks with
Peanut Butter, 226
-Honey Doughnuts, 225
-Lemon Macaroons, 176

Milk, 195
milk, buying, 25
Milk, Quick, 195
Milk and Lemongrass Infusion,
Tom Yum Kai with, 62
and Papaya, Banana
Leaf–Wrapped Halibut with,
100
Toasted, 53
Toasted, and Papaya, Thai Beef
Salad with, 52–53
coffee, in SCD, 22
cookies:
Lemon-Coconut Macaroons,
176
Orange and Almond Flour,
173
corn, in SCD, 21
couscous, in SCD, 21
crème fraîche:
Homemade, 28
Vodka-and-Honey-Cured
Salmon with, 42
cucumber(s):
and Celery Boats with Herbed
Farmer Cheese, 217
Fresh Spring Rolls with Spicy
Chile Dipping Sauce, 34
Gazpacho, 69
Raita, 88
Soup, Chilled, with Yogurt and
Dill, 67
Cumin-Garlic Yogurt, 123
currant(s):
Curried Celery Rémoulade, 43
-Mango Chutney, 37
Saffron, and Cashews,
Moroccan Chicken Stew
with, 110–11
Scones with Apricot Butter,
204
curried dishes:
Curried Celery Rémoulade, 43
Curried Deviled Eggs with
Mango-Currant Chutney, 36
Green Chicken Curry with Kaffir
Limes and Lemongrass,
112–13
Tilapia Curry with Saffron,
96–97
Yogurt Curry Dip, 83
Curry Paste, 112–13

**D**

dairy products. *See also* cheese;
yogurt
allowed in SCD, 21
buying, for yogurt making, 26
date(s):
-Barbecue Sauce, 124–25
Ice Cream, 184
Lamb Keftas with Yogurt Dip,
130
Medjool, buying, 25
Medjool, Macadamia Cake, 177
desserts and confections:
Banana Boats, 224
Coconut Cake, 174–75
Date Ice Cream, 184
Frozen Banana Sticks with
Peanut Butter, 226
Herb Candies, 185
Honey-Coconut Doughnuts,
225
Lemon-Coconut Macaroons,
176
Macadamia Medjool Date Cake,
177
Macadamia Nut Brittle, 181
Orange and Almond Flour
Cookies, 173
Peach Pocket Pies, 222–23
Peanut Butter Toffees, 182
Persimmon Cream Cups, 180
Strawberry Ice Cream, 184
Tarte Tatin, 178–79
Whipped Cashew Cream, 183
dips and spreads:
Aïoli, 82
Artichoke Dip, 86
Carrot-Ginger Paste, 78
Cucumber Raita, 88
Hollandaise Sauce, 77
Homemade Dijon Mustard, 80
Honey Mustard, 81
Horseradish Mustard, 81
Lamb Keftas with Yogurt Dip,
130
Lemon Garlic Mustard, 81
Lemon-Onion Dip, 40–41
Lucques Olive Tapenade, 87
Orange Honey Butter, 210
Roasted Red Pepper Spread,
79